M000309979

Remember This?

People, Things and Events
FROM **1950** TO THE **PRESENT DAY**

US EDITION

With thanks for additional research by Larry Farr,
Dana Lemay, Rose Myers and Idan Solon.

Baby statistics: Office of Retirement and Disability Policy,
Social Security Administration.

Cover: Library of Congress: New York World-Telegram and the Sun
Newspaper Photograph Collection / LC-DIG-ds-00970;
Mary Evans: Glasshouse Images, Everett Collection, Keystone Pictures
USA/zumapress.com. Icons: rawpixel/Freepik.

Cover Design: Fanni Williams / thehappycolourstudio.com

The Milestone Memories series including this *Remember This?*
title is produced by Milestones Memories Press, a division
of Say So Media Ltd.

First edition: October 2021
Updated: February 2022

We've tried our best to check our facts, but mistakes can still slip through.
Spotted one? We'd love to know about it: info@saysomedia.net

Rewind, Replay, Remember

What can you remember before you turned six? If you're like most of us, not much: the comforting smell of a blanket or the rough texture of a sweater, perhaps. A mental snapshot of a parent arriving home late at night. A tingle of delight or the shadow of sorrow.

But as we grow out of childhood, our autobiographical and episodic memories—they're the ones hitched to significant events such as birthdays or leaving school—are created and filed more effectively, enabling us to piece them together at a later date. And the more we revisit those memories, the less likely we are to lose the key that unlocks them.

We assemble these fragments into a more-or-less coherent account of our lives—the one we tell to ourselves, our friends, our relatives. And while this one-of-a-kind biopic loses a little definition over the years, some episodes remain in glorious technicolor—although it's usually the most embarrassing incidents!

But this is one movie that's never quite complete. Have you ever had a memory spring back unbidden, triggered by something seemingly unrelated? This book is an attempt to discover those forgotten scenes using the events, sounds, and faces linked to the milestones in your life.

It's time to blow off the cobwebs and see how much you can remember!

It Happened in 1950

The biggest event in the year is one that didn't make the front pages: you were born! Here are some of the national stories that people were talking about.

+ Attempted assassination of President Truman
+ Boston's Great Brink's Robbery occurs
+ Shirley Temple retires (aged 22)
+ FCC issues first license to broadcast TV in color
+ James Dean appears in commercial
+ Great Appalachian Storm hits
+ Peanuts comic strip published
+ California celebrates its centennial
+ Beetle Bailey comic strip created
+ US military to aid defense of South Korea
+ National Council of Churches formed
+ Russian spy Harry Gold arrested by FBI (right)
+ Truman signs Guam Act
+ First TV remote control offered for sale
+ Diner's Club issues first credit card
+ Black player drafted into NBA
+ Brooklyn-Battery Tunnel opens
+ Men's National Soccer team defeats England in FIFA World Cup
+ Antihistamines sold as cold-relief medications
+ L. Ron Hubbard publishes Dianetics
+ Laws passed to restrict communists and communist parties

Born this year:
රූ Singer Stevie Wonder
රූ Entertainer Jay Leno
රූ Senator Chuck Schumer

Harry Gold, seen here in 1950 after his arrest by the FBI, was one link in a chain of spies responsible for passing details of the Manhattan Project to the Soviet Union. A Jell-O boxtop was torn in half and used by Gold as an identifying "passport" during one clandestine meeting. Sentenced to 30 years, he became a government witness and helped convict others, including the Rosenbergs (executed for espionage in 1953). Gold was released in 1965.

On the Bookshelf When You Were Small

The books of our childhood linger long in the memory. These are the children's classics, all published in your first ten years. Do you remember the stories? What about the covers?

1950	Better Known as Johnny Appleseed by Mabel Leigh Hunt
1950	The Lion, the Witch and the Wardrobe by C.S. Lewis
1951	Ginger Pye by Eleanor Estes
1951	The Wailing Siren Mystery by Franklin W. Dixon
1951	Prince Caspian: The Return to Narnia by C.S. Lewis
1952	Five Little Monkeys by Juliet Kepes
1952	Charlotte's Web by E.B. White
1952	The Borrowers by Mary Norton
1953	The Little Red Caboose by Marian Potter
1953	...And Now, Miguel by Joseph Krumgold
1954	Cinderella, or the Little Glass Slipper by Marcia Brown
1954	Book of Nursery and Mother Goose Rhymes by Marguerite de Angeli
1955	**Harold and the Purple Crayon by Crockett Johnson** **Harold's author was cartoonist David Johnson Leisk (he thought Crockett would be easier to say). He worked with his wife, Ruth Krauss, on the 1945 bestseller The Carrot Seed, and his interest in mathematics led him to create geometric paintings which now hang in the National Museum of American History.**
1955	Beezus and Ramona by Beverly Cleary
1955	Eloise by Kay Thompson
1956	The Hundred and One Dalmatians by Dodie Smith
1956	Old Yeller by Fred Gipson
1957	Little Bear by Else Holmelund Minarik
1957	The Cat in the Hat by Dr. Seuss
1958	The Witch of Blackbird Pond by Elizabeth George Speare
1958	A Bear Called Paddington by Michael Bond
1958	The House That Jack Built by Antonio Frasconi
1959	The Rescuers by Margery Sharp
1959	My Side of the Mountain by Jean George

Around the World in Your Birth Year

Here are the events from outside the US that were big enough to make news back home in the year you were born. And you won't remember any of them!

✦ Nations recognize People's Republic of China
✦ Earthquake and floods devastate India
✦ UK ends 11-year-long gas rationing
✦ Volcanic cloud kills thousands in New Guinea
✦ Warsaw Pact is formed
✦ China invades Tibet
✦ Turing tests how machines can imitate humans
✦ Jordan annexes the West Bank
✦ South Africa officially segregates races by areas
✦ Viet Minh troops attack French soldiers
✦ Volkswagen Minibus is produced
✦ Egypt demands UK leave Suez Canal region
✦ Tollund Man is discovered
✦ Florence Chadwick completes first leg of both-ways English Channel crossing
✦ Pope Pius XII declares evolution a serious hypothesis
✦ Korean War begins
✦ Australia uses myxomatosis to control rabbits
✦ FIA Formula One Championship run
✦ Uruguay wins World Cup
✦ East Germany forms the Stasi
✦ West Germany expunges communist officials
✦ India forms a republic
✦ Soviet Union and PRC sign mutual defense treaty
✦ Belgium holds referendum on monarchy
✦ France imposes minimum wage

Boys' Names When You Were Born

Once upon a time, popular names came… and stuck. (John hogged the top spot for 40 years, to 1924.) These are the most popular names when you were born.

James
James was not only the first choice in 1950, it was the most popular boy's name of the last hundred years, bestowed upon nearly five million babies (narrowly beating John into second place).

Robert
John
Michael
David
William
Richard
Thomas
Charles
Gary
Larry
Ronald
Joseph
Donald
Kenneth
Steven
Dennis
Paul
Stephen
George
Daniel
Edward
Mark
Jerry
Gregory

Rising and falling stars:
Eric appeared in the Top 100 for the first time this year.

Girls' Names When You Were Born

On the girls' side of the maternity ward, Mary held the crown in every year from 1880 to 1946—and she'd be back on top by 1953 for a further nine years.

Linda

Mary

After topping the list for nearly 70 years, it's perhaps unsurprising that Mary's fall from popularity was slow and graceful. She only left the Top 100 in 2008.

Patricia

Barbara

Susan

Nancy

In sixth place, this was Nancy's best ever ranking.

Deborah

Sandra

Carol

Kathleen

Sharon

Karen

Donna

Brenda

Margaret

Diane

Pamela

Janet

Shirley

Carolyn

Judith

Janice

Cynthia

Elizabeth

Judy

Rising and falling stars:

While Irene, Joann and Sue dropped out of the Top 100 for good, Debra and Denise were fresh faces.

Things People Did When You Were Growing Up...

...that hardly anyone does now. Some of these we remember fondly; others are best left in the past!

- ✦ Help Mom make cookies using a cookie press
- ✦ Keep bread in a breadbox
- ✦ Can and preserve vegetables from your garden
- ✦ Listen to daytime soap operas on the radio
- ✦ Participate in Church fundraisers
- ✦ Watch endurance competitions like flagpole sitting and goldfish eating
- ✦ Build scooters from roller skates and scrap wood
- ✦ Bring a slide-rule to math class
- ✦ Take a Sunday drive out to the country
- ✦ Play leapfrog
- ✦ Live in a Sears Modern Home ordered from the Sears catalog
- ✦ Get a treat from the pharmacy soda fountain
- ✦ Camp in a "Hooverville" while looking for work
- ✦ Keep a thrift or kitchen garden
- ✦ Buy penny candy
- ✦ Buy goods from door-to-door salesmen
- ✦ Wear clothing made from flour sacks
- ✦ Collect marbles
- ✦ Join a dance marathon
- ✦ Listen to Amos n' Andy on the radio on weekend evenings
- ✦ Eat Water Pie
- ✦ "Window shop" downtown on Saturdays
- ✦ Pitch pennies
- ✦ Earn $30 a month plus food and shelter working for the Civilian Conservation Corps

How Many of These Games Are Still Played?

The first half of the 20th century was the heyday for new board and card games launched to the US public. Some are still firm family favorites, but which ones did you play when you were young?

1925	Pegity
1925	Playing for the Cup
1927	Hokum ("The game for a roomful")
1920s	The Greyhound Racing Game
1930	Wahoo
1932	Finance
1934	Sorry!
1935	**Monopoly**

1935   **Monopoly**
The game's origins lie with The Landlord's Game, patented in 1904 by Elizabeth Magie. (The anti-monopoly version–Prosperity–didn't catch on.) It was the first game with a never-ending path rather than a fixed start and finish.

1935	Easy Money
1936	The Amazing Adventures of Fibber McGee
1937	Meet the Missus
1937	Stock Ticker
1938	Scrabble
1938	Movie Millions
1940	Dig
1940	Prowl Car
1942	Sea Raider
1943	Chutes and Ladders
1949	**Clue**

1949   **Clue**
Clue–or Cluedo, as it is known to most outside the USA–introduced us to a host of shady characters and grisly murder weapons. For years those included a piece of genuine lead pipe, now replaced on health grounds.

1949   **Candy Land**
This wholesome family racing game, invented on a polio ward, was the victim of something less savory nearly 50 years after its launch when an adult website claimed the domain name. Thankfully, the courts swiftly intervened.

Things People Do Now...

...that were virtually unknown when you were young. How many of these habits are part of your routine or even second nature these days? Do you remember the first time?

- ✦ Get curbside grocery pickup
- ✦ Stream movies instead of going to Blockbuster for a rental
- ✦ Learn remotely and online
- ✦ Communicate by text or video chat
- ✦ Use a Kindle or other e-reading device
- ✦ Go geocaching
- ✦ Track your sleep, exercise, or fertility with a watch
- ✦ Use a weighted blanket
- ✦ Use a robotic/automatic vacuum
- ✦ Take your dog to a dog park
- ✦ Have a package delivered by drone
- ✦ Find a date online or through an app
- ✦ Use hand sanitizer
- ✦ Automatically soothe your baby with a self-rocking bassinet
- ✦ Host a gender-reveal party during pregnancy
- ✦ Use a home essential oil diffuser or salt lamp
- ✦ Have a "destination wedding"
- ✦ Use a device charging station while waiting for a flight
- ✦ Get a ride from Uber or Lyft instead of a taxi
- ✦ Drink hard seltzer
- ✦ Take a home DNA test (for you... or your pet)
- ✦ Have a telemedicine/virtual healthcare visit
- ✦ Smoke an e-cigarette/"vape"
- ✦ Start your car, dryer, or air conditioner via an app

Popular Food in the 1950s

For many, the post-war years meant more of one thing in particular on the table: meat. In the yard, men stepped up to the barbeque to sharpen their skills. In the kitchen, fancy new electric appliances and frozen TV dinners promised convenience and new, exotic flavors.

Tuna noodle casserole

Dinty Moore Beef Stew

Beef stroganoff

Green bean casserole

Green bean casserole was invented in the Campbell's test kitchen in 1955 as a cheap, fuss-free dish. Today, around 40 percent of Campbell's Cream of Mushroom soup sold in the US goes into this dinner table staple.

Pigs-in-a-blanket

Pigs get different blankets in the United Kingdom, where sausages are wrapped in bacon rather than pastry.

Backyard barbecues

Ovaltine

Swedish meatballs

Pineapple upside down cake

Spam

Ground pork shoulder and ham sold in a distinctive can—for much of the world, that means Spam. This "meatloaf without basic training" is affordable and still popular, with over eight billion cans sold since it was first sold in 1937.

Ambrosia salad

Sugar Smacks

Cheez Whiz

Stuffed celery

Campbell's Tomato Soup spice cake

Swanson Turkey TV Dinners

Dreamed up as a solution to an over-supply of turkey, TV dinners proved nearly as popular as the TV itself. Swanson sold over 25 million of them in 1954, the year these handy meal packs were launched.

Veg-All canned vegetables

Chicken à la King

Cars of the 1950s

Was this the golden age of automobiles? In truth, some of these models had been brought to market long before, such as the Buick Roadmaster and the Studebaker Champion. But even stalwarts were quick to adopt the Space Age theme of the decade as sweeping lines, tailfins, and cascading chrome grilles became the norm.

1926	Chrysler Imperial
1936	General Motors Buick Roadmaster
1939	**Studebaker Champion** Over seven decades, the Champion's creator, Raymond Loewy, designed railroads, logos, buses, vending machines, and a space station for NASA.
1939	Chrysler DeSoto Custom
1947	Studebaker Starlight Coupe
1948	**Crosley Station Wagon** The first car to be marketed as "Sports Utility."
1948	Jaguar XK120
1949	**Muntz Jet** Fewer than 200 Muntz Jets were built by founder Madman Muntz, an engineer who married seven times and made (and lost) fortunes selling cars, TVs, and more.
1949	Chrysler Dodge Coronet
1950	General Motors Chevrolet Bel-Air
1950	Nash Rambler
1951	Hudson Hornet
1953	General Motors Chevrolet Corvette
1953	General Motors Buick Skylark
1953	General Motors Cadillac Eldorado
1953	Nash Metropolitan
1954	Ford Skyliner
1955	Ford Thunderbird
1955	Ford Fairlane
1956	Studebaker Golden Hawk
1956	Chrysler Plymouth Fury
1957	**Mercedes-Benz 300 SL Roadster** Voted "Sports Car of the Century" in 1999.

Cars crawl out of 1950s Philadelphia over the Ben Franklin Bridge. Henry Ford wasn't the only one to "build a car for the great multitude." Millions of new suburbanites embraced their newfound freedom—even if that meant driving to the same place as everyone else.

The Biggest Hits When You Were 10

Whistled by your father, hummed by your sister or overheard on the radio, these are the hit records as you reached double digits.

Sam Cooke ♪ Chain Gang
Connie Francis ♪ Everybody's Somebody's Fool
Roy Orbison ♪ Only the Lonely
Chubby Checker ♪ The Twist
Jimmy Jones ♪ Handyman
The Drifters ♪ Save the Last Dance for Me
The Shirelles ♪ Will You Love Me Tomorrow
Ray Charles ♪ Georgia on My Mind
The Hollywood Argyles ♪ Alley Oop
The Everly Brothers ♪ Cathy's Clown
Ferlin Husky ♪ Wings of a Dove
Percy Faith and His Orchestra ♪ Theme from A Summer Place
Brian Hyland ♪ Itsy Bitsy Teenie Weenie Yellow
Polkadot Bikini
Brook Benton ♪ Kiddio
Jim Reeves ♪ He'll Have to Go
The Ventures ♪ Walk, Don't Run
Brenda Lee ♪ I'm Sorry
Jackie Wilson ♪ Doggin' Around
The Miracles ♪ Shop Around
Loretta Lynn ♪ I'm a Honky Tonk Girl
Dinah Washington
and Brook Benton ♪ Baby (You've Got What it Takes)
Hank Locklin ♪ Please Help Me, I'm Falling
Edith Piaf ♪ Milord
Paul Anka ♪ Puppy Love

Faster, Easier, Better

Yesterday's technological breakthrough is today's modern convenience. Here are some of the lab and engineering marvels that were made before you turned 21 years old.

1950	Teleprompter
1951	Wetsuit
1952	Artificial heart
1953	Heart-lung machine
1954	Acoustic suspension loudspeaker
1955	Pocket transistor radio
1956	Hard Disk Drive
1956	Operating system (OS)
1957	Laser
1958	Microchip
1959	Weather satellite
1960	Global navigation satellite system
1961	Spreadsheet (electronic)
1962	Red LED
1963	**Computer mouse**

The inventor of the computer mouse had patented it in 1963. However, by the time the mouse became commercially available in the 1980s, his patent had expired. The first computer system that made use of a (giant) mouse came from Xerox in 1981.

1964	Plasma display
1965	Hypertext (http)
1966	Computer RAM
1967	Hand-held calculator
1968	Virtual Reality
1969	Laser printer
1970	**Wireless local area network**

The first wireless local network was developed by the University of Hawaii to communicate data among the Hawaiian Islands.

Across the Nation

Double digits at last: you're old enough to eavesdrop on adults and scan the headlines. These may be some of the earliest national news stories you remember.

+ Birth control pill approved
+ Lucille Ball divorces Desi Arnaz
+ John F. Kennedy elected president
+ USAF captain sets three parachute records from 100,000 feet
+ Arnold Palmer wins US Open
+ Actress Joanne Woodward given first Hollywood star
+ Laser patented—and 30-year dispute begins
+ Domino's Pizza opens in Michigan
+ Woolworth's lunch counter sit-in occurs
+ Civil Rights Acts of 1960 signed
+ Wilt Chamberlain sets record as 7'1" rookie in NBA
+ Wilma Rudolph wins three gold medals in 1960 Olympics
+ Cassius Clay "floats like a butterfly" to become heavyweight champ
+ Aluminum cans first used, for frozen juice
+ U-2 pilot captured by Soviet Union
+ New Orleans desegregation crisis begins
+ Pioneer 5 launched to map interplanetary magnetic field
+ Supreme Court decides Boynton v. Virginia
+ Nuclear-powered USS Enterprise launched
+ Winter Olympics hosted in California
+ Etch A Sketch goes on sale
+ The Twist becomes dance craze
+ US Hockey team wins gold medal
+ Pittsburgh Pirates win the World Series

Born this year:
& Apple CEO Tim Cook
& Actor Sean Penn
& John F. Kennedy Jr.

Kapow! Comic Books and Heroes from Your Childhood

Barely a year went past in the mid-20th Century without a new super-powered hero arriving to save the day. Here are some that were taking on the bad guys during your childhood.

Rawhide Kid ✳ Rawhide Kid
Showcase ✳ Barry Allen
World's Finest Comics ✳ Superman
Patsy Walker ✳ Patsy Walker
Kid Colt, Outlaw ✳ Kid Colt
Mickey Mouse ✳ Mickey Mouse
Adventure Comics ✳ Aquaman
The Flash ✳ Wally West
Green Lantern ✳ Hal Jordan
Richie Rich ✳ Richie Rich
G.I. Combat ✳ The Haunted Tank
Donald Duck ✳ Donald Duck
Fantastic Four ✳ The Thing
Tales To Astonish ✳ Ant-Man
Uncle Scrooge ✳ Uncle Scrooge
The Incredible Hulk ✳ Hulk
The Avengers ✳ Thor
Wonder Woman ✳ Wonder Woman
The Amazing Spider-Man ✳ Spider-Man
Detective Comics ✳ Batman
Daredevil ✳ Daredevil
The X-Men ✳ X-Men
Tales of Suspense ✳ Captain America
Sgt. Fury & His Howling Commandos ✳ **Nick Fury**

The title was chosen as a bet: co-creator Stan Lee reckoned that he and Jack Kirby could find success with a silly name—and they did just that.

Winners of the Stanley Cup Since You Were Born

The prestigious Stanley Cup has been changing hands since 1893, although the trophy itself has been redesigned more than once. Here are the teams to lift the champagne-filled cup since you were born.

- **Detroit Red Wings (8)**
  1955: 18-year-old Larry Hillman became the youngest player to have his name engraved on the Stanley Cup trophy.

- Chicago Black Hawks (4)

- **Boston Bruins (3)**
  1970: Bobby Orr scored perhaps the most famous goal in NHL history, in midair, to clinch the title.

- **New York Rangers (1)**
  After a 1940 victory, the Rangers would not win another Stanley Cup for another 54 years.

- Toronto Maple Leafs (5)
- Montreal Canadiens (18)
- Philadelphia Flyers (2)
- New York Islanders (4)
- Edmonton Oilers (5)

- **Calgary Flames (1)**
  1989 was the last time a Stanley Cup Final has been played between two teams from Canada.

- Pittsburgh Penguins (5)
- New Jersey Devils (3)

- **Colorado Avalanche (2)**
  1996: A win in their first season after moving from Quebec (where their nickname was the Nordiques).

- Dallas Stars (1)
- Tampa Bay Lightning (3)
- Carolina Hurricanes (1)
- Anaheim Ducks (1)
- Los Angeles Kings (2)
- Washington Capitals (1)
- St. Louis Blues (1)

On the Silver Screen When You Were 11

From family favorites to the films you weren't allowed to watch, these are the films and actors that drew the praise and the crowds when you turned 11.

101 Dalmatians  Rod Taylor, Cate Bauer, Betty Lou Gerson

The Misfits  Clark Gable, Marilyn Monroe, Montgomery Clift

The Absent Minded Professor  Fred MacMurray, Nancy Olson, Tommy Kirk

Judgment at Nuremberg  Spencer Tracy, Burt Lancaster, Richard Widmark

La Dolce Vita  Marcello Mastroianni, Anita Ekberg, Anouk Aimee

Saturday Night and Sunday Morning  Albert Finney, Shirley Annie Field, Rachel Roberts

Rocco and His Brothers  Alain Delon, Renato Salvatori, Annie Girardot

Black Sunday  Barbara Steele, John Richardson, Andrea Checchi

Return to Peyton Place  Carol Lynley, Tuesday Weld, Jeff Chandler
Diane Varsi was recruited to play Allison MacKenzie, but she retired.

Kumonosu  Toshiro Mifune, Isuzu Yamada, Takashi Shimura

The Parent Trap  Hayley Mills, Maureen O'Hara, Brian Keith

The Guns of Navarone  Gregory Peck, David Niven, Anthony Quinn

Fanny  Leslie Caron, Horst Buchholz, Maurice Chevalier
Audrey Hepburn was originally cast as Fanny, but subsequently turned down the role.

El Cid  Charlton Heston, Sophia Loren, Raf Vallone

Come September  Rock Hudson, Gina Lollobrigida, Sandra Dee

A Woman is a Woman  Jean-Claude Brialy, Anna Karina

Lover Come Back  Rock Hudson, Doris Day, Tony Randall

The Hustler  Paul Newman, Jackie Gleason, Piper Laurie

Breakfast at Tiffany's  Audrey Hepburn, George Peppard, Patricia Neal

West Side Story  Natalie Wood, Richard Beymer, Rita Moreno

King of Kings  Jeffrey Hunter, Siobhan McKenna, Robert Ryan

Flower Drum Song  Nancy Kwan, James Shigeta, Miyoshi Umeki

Splendor in the Grass  Natalie Wood, Warren Beatty, Pat Hingle

Babes in Toyland  Ray Bolger, Tommy Sands, Annette Funicello

Comic Strips You'll Know

Comic strips took off in the late 19th century and for much of the 20th century they were a dependable feature of everyday life. Some were solo efforts; others became so-called zombie strips, living on well beyond their creator. A century on, some are still going. But how many from your youth will you remember?

1940-52	The Spirit by Will Eisner
1930-	**Blondie** In 1995, Blondie was one of 20 strips commemorated by the US Postal Service in the Comic Strip Classics series.
1931-	**Dick Tracy** Gould's first idea? A detective called Plainclothes Tracy.
1930-95	Mickey Mouse
1932-	Mary Worth
1936-	**The Phantom** Lee Falk worked on The Phantom for 63 years and Mandrake The Magician for 65.
1919-	Barney Google and Snuffy Smith
1938-	Nancy
1946-	Mark Trail
1937-	**Prince Valiant** Edward, the Duke of Windsor (previously Edward VIII), called Prince Valiant the "greatest contribution to English literature in the past hundred years."
1934-2003	**Flash Gordon** Alex Raymond created Flash Gordon to compete with the Buck Rogers comic strip.
1934-77	Li'l Abner by Al Capp
1925-74	Etta Kett by Paul Robinson
1947-69	Grandma by Charles Kuhn
1948-	Rex Morgan, M.D.
1933-87	Brick Bradford
1950-2000	**Peanuts by Charles M. Schulz** Schultz was inducted into the Hockey Hall of Fame after building the Redwood Empire Arena near his studio.
1950-	Beetle Bailey

Biggest Hits by The King

He may have conquered rock'n'roll, but Elvis's success straddled genres including country music, R&B, and more. These are his Number 1s from across the charts, beginning with the rockabilly "I Forgot…" through the posthumous country hit, "Guitar Man."

I Forgot to Remember to Forget (1955)
Heartbreak Hotel (1956)
I Want You, I Need You, I Love You (1956)
Don't Be Cruel (1956)
Hound Dog (1956)
Love Me Tender (1956)
Too Much (1957)
All Shook Up (1957)
(Let Me Be Your) Teddy Bear (1957)
Jailhouse Rock (1957)
Don't (1957)
Wear My Ring Around Your Neck (1958)
Hard Headed Woman (1958)
A Big Hunk O' Love (1959)
Stuck On You (1960)
It's Now or Never (1960)
Are You Lonesome Tonight? (1960)
Surrender (1961)
Good Luck Charm (1962)
Suspicious Minds (1969)
Moody Blue (1976)
Way Down (1977)
Guitar Man (1981)

Childhood Candies

In labs across the country, mid-century food scientists dreamed up new and colorful ways to delight children just like you. These are the fruits of their labor, launched before you turned twenty-one.

1950	Cup-O-Gold (Hoffman Candy Company)
1950	Red Vines (American Licorice Co.)
1950	Hot Tamales (Just Born)
1950	Rocky Road Candy Bar (The Annabell Candy Co.)
1952	Pixy Stix (Sunline, Inc.)
1954	Atomic Fireballs (Ferrera Candy Co.)
1954	**Marshmallow Peeps** (Just Born) Today it takes six minutes to make one Peep, but when the candy was first introduced, it took 27 hours!
1954	Peanut M&Ms (Mars)
1955	**Chick-O-Sticks** (Atkinson's) These candies were called "Chicken Bones" until they were renamed in 1955.
1950s	Swedish Fish (Malaco)
1950s	Look! Candy Bar (Golden Nugget Candy Co.)
1960	Sixlets (Leaf Brands)
1962	Now and Later (Phoenix Candy Company)
1962	SweeTarts (Sunline, Inc.)
1962	LemonHead (Ferrara Candy Company)
1963	**Cadbury Creme Eggs** (Fry's) An original 1963 Fry's Creme Egg (as they were then called) was discovered in 2017. It hasn't been eaten.
1964	100 Grand Bar (Nestle)
1960s	Spree (Sunline Candy Company)
1966	Razzles (Fleer)
1967	**M&M Fruit Chewies** (Mars) In 1960, Mars launched "Opal Fruits" in the UK, possibly after a competition entry from a boy named Peter. Seven years later, they appeared in the US as Starburst. It took 20 years for the name to be standardized worldwide.
1968	Caramello Bar (Cadbury)

Books of the Decade

Ten years of your life that took you from adventure books aged 10 to dense works of profundity at 20—or perhaps just grown-up adventures! How many did you read when they were first published?

1960	To Kill a Mockingbird by Harper Lee
1960	Hawaii by James Michener
1961	Catch-22 by Joseph Heller
1961	Stranger in a Strange Land by Robert A. Heinlein
1962	One Flew Over the Cuckoo's Nest by Ken Kesey
1962	Franny and Zooey by J.D. Salinger
1963	The Bell Jar by Sylvia Plath
1963	The Feminine Mystique by Betty Friedan
1963	A Clockwork Orange by Anthony Burgess
1964	The Group by Mary McCarthy
1964	Herzog by Saul Bellow
1964	The Spy Who Came in from the Cold by John le Carré
1964	Up the Down Staircase by Bel Kaufman
1965	Dune by Frank Herbert
1966	Valley of the Dolls by Jacqueline Susann
1966	In Cold Blood by Truman Capote
1967	Rosemary's Baby by Ira Levin
1967	The Arrangement by Elia Kazan
1967	The Confessions of Nat Turner by William Styron
1968	Airport by Arthur Hailey
1968	Couples by John Updike
1969	The Godfather by Mario Puzo
1969	Slaughterhouse-Five by Kurt Vonnegut
1969	Portnoy's Complaint by Philip Roth
1969	The French Lieutenant's Woman by John Fowles

US Buildings

Some were loathed then, loved now; others, the reverse. Some broke new architectural ground; others housed famous or infamous businesses, or helped to power a nation. All of them were built in your first 18 years.

1950	Metropolitan Life North Building
1951	US General Accounting Office Building
1952	United Nations Secretariat Building
1953	Sullivan Tower, Nashville
1954	Republic Center, Dallas
1955	One Prudential Plaza, Chicago
1956	**Capitol Records Building, Los Angeles** The world's first circular office building.
1957	666 Fifth Avenue, New York City
1958	Time & Life Building, New York City
1959	2 Broadway, New York City
1960	Four Gateway Center, Pittsburgh
1961	One Chase Manhattan Plaza
1962	Kennedy Space Center, Florida
1963	**MetLife Building, New York City** The largest office space in the world when it opened, the MetLife was born as the Pan Am Building, complete with heliport and 15 ft. lit signage atop (the last permitted).
1964	277 Park Avenue, New Yor City
1965	Cheyenne Mountain complex, Colorado
1966	John F. Kennedy Federal Building, Boston
1967	Watergate Hotel and Office Complex
1968	**John Hancock Center, Chicago** Second-highest in the world when it opened, the tower is still a creditable 33rd tallest when measured to the tip of its antenna.

Radio DJs from Your Childhood

If the radio was the soundtrack to your life as you grew up, some of these voices were part of the family. (The stations listed are where these DJs made their name; the dates are their radio broadcasting career).

Wolfman Jack 🎙 XERB/Armed Forces Radio (1960–1995)
Jocko Henderson 🎙 WDAS/W LIB (1952–1991)
Casey Kasem 🎙 KRLA (1954–2010)
Kasem was the host of American Top 40 for four decades.
By 1986, his show was broadcast on 1,000 radio stations.

Bruce Morrow 🎙 WABC (1959–)
Murray Kaufman 🎙 WINS (1958–1975)
You'll likely remember him as Murray the K, the self-declared "fifth Beatle" (he played a lot of music from the Fab Four).

Alison Steele 🎙 WNEW-FM (1966–1995)
Aka The Nightbird, Steele was that rarity of the sixties and seventies: a successful female DJ.

Alan Freed 🎙 WJW/WINS (1945–1965)
Freed's career crashed after he was found to have been taking payola. His contribution was recognized posthumously when admitted into the Rock n Roll Hall of Fame.

Robert W. Morgan 🎙 KHJ-AM (1955–1998)
Dan Ingram 🎙 WABC (1958–2004)
Dave Hull 🎙 KRLA (1955–2010)
Another candidate for the "fifth Beatle," Hull interviewed the band many times.

Hal Jackson 🎙 WBLS (1940–2011)
Johnny Holliday 🎙 KYA (1956–)
Herb Kent 🎙 WVON (1944–2016)
"Cool Gent" Herb Kent was the longest-serving DJ on the radio.

Tom Donahue 🎙 WIBG/KYA (1949–1975)
John R. 🎙 WLAC (1941–1973)
Bill Randle 🎙 WERE/WCBS (1940s–2004)
Jack Spector 🎙 WMCA (1955–1994)
Spector, one of WMCA's "Good Guys," died on air in 1994.
A long silence after playing "I'm in the Mood for Love" alerted station staff.

It Happened in 1966

Here's a round-up of the most newsworthy events from across the US in the year you turned (sweet) 16.

+ Kevlar invented
+ John Lennon's "Jesus" comment sparks outrage
+ Uniform Time Act signed
+ Supreme Court decides Miranda v. Arizona
+ National Organization for Women founded
+ Richard Speck murders eight nurses
+ Charles Whitman commits murder from atop UT tower
+ Caesars Palace opens in Las Vegas
+ Actor Ronald Reagan elected governor of California
+ First Kwanzaa celebrated
+ Department of Transportation established
+ Quaker Instant Oatmeal introduced
+ NASA completes several Gemini missions
+ Draft Deferment Test given
+ Race riots across Atlanta and other US cities
+ First black member of President's cabinet appointed (Robert C. Weaver)
+ Pro football game with the highest score ever played
+ Artificial heart implanted
+ Grenada school segregation protests (right)
+ Medicare takes effect
+ Walt Disney died
+ Billie Jean King wins Wimbledon
+ The Met moves to the Lincoln Center
+ Two national football leagues to merge into one entity

Born this year:
- Singer Janet Jackson
- Actor David Schwimmer
- Model Cindy Crawford

September 1966: Martin Luther King escorts children to school in Grenada, Mississippi. A federal judge had given the go-ahead for African American children to enroll in schools that were still segregated despite the Supreme Court ruling 12 years before. The delayed start of term had been marred by violence and threats against the new children and their families before belated

News Anchors of the Fifties and Sixties

Trusted, familiar, and exclusively male: these are the faces that brought you the news, and the catchphrases they made their own.

Edward R. Murrow 📺 CBS (1938-59)
"Good night, and good luck."

Walter Cronkite 📺 CBS (1962-81)
"And that's the way it is."

David Brinkley 📺 NBC (1956-71)
"Good night, Chet..."

Chet Huntley 📺 NBC (1956-70)
"...Good night, David."

Harry Reasoner 📺 CBS & ABC (1961-91)

Frank Reynolds 📺 ABC (1968-70)

John Charles Daly 📺 CBS & ABC (1941-60)
"Good night and a good tomorrow."

Douglas Edwards 📺 CBS (1948-62)

Hugh Downs 📺 NBC (1962-71)

John Chancellor 📺 NBC (1970-82)

Paul Harvey 📺 ABC Radio (1951-2009)
"Hello Americans, this is Paul Harvey. Stand by for news!"

Mike Wallace 📺 CBS (1963-66)

John Cameron Swayze 📺 NBC (1948-56)
"Well, that's the story, folks! This is John Cameron Swayze, and I'm glad we could get together."

Ron Cochran 📺 ABC (1962-65)

Bob Young 📺 ABC (1967-68)

Dave Garroway 📺 NBC (1952-61)

Bill Shadel 📺 ABC (1960-63)

Fifties Game Shows

It all started so well: appointment radio became appointment TV, with new and crossover game shows bringing us together. But as the decade progressed, the scandal emerged: some shows were fixed. Quiz shows were down, but certainly not out. (Dates include periods off-air.)

Break the Bank 🏆 (1945–57)
Beat The Clock 🏆 (1950–2019)
Name That Tune 🏆 (1952–85)
A radio crossover that spawned 25 international versions.

Strike It Rich 🏆 (1947–58)
The Price Is Right 🏆 (1956–65)
The original version of the current quiz that began in 1972. This one was hosted by Bill Cullen.

Down You Go 🏆 (1951–56)
I've Got A Secret 🏆 (1952–2006)
What's The Story 🏆 (1951–55)
The $64,000 Question 🏆 (1955–58)
People Are Funny 🏆 (1942–60)
Tic-Tac-Dough 🏆 (1956–90)
Early Tic-Tac-Dough contestants were often coached; around three-quarters of the shows in one run were rigged.

The Name's The Same 🏆 (1951–55)
Two For The Money 🏆 (1952–57)
The Big Payoff 🏆 (1951–62)
Twenty-One 🏆 (1956–58)
At the heart of the rigging scandal, Twenty-One was the subject of Robert Redford's 1994 movie, Quiz Show.

Masquerade Party 🏆 (1952–60)
You Bet Your Life 🏆 (1947–61)
A comedy quiz hosted by Groucho Marx.

Truth or Consequences 🏆 (1940–88)
Started life as a radio quiz. TV host Bob Barker signed off with: "Hoping all your consequences are happy ones."

20 Questions 🏆 (1946–55)
What's My Line 🏆 (1950–75)

Liberty Issue Stamps

First released in 1954, the Liberty Issue drew its name from not one but three depictions of the Statue of Liberty across the denominations. (There was only room for one "real" woman, though.) It coincided with the new era of stamp collecting as a childhood hobby that endured for decades. Were you one of these new miniature philatelists?

Benjamin Franklin ½ ¢ Polymath (writer, inventor, scientist)
Franklin discovered the principle of electricity,
the Law of Conservation of Charge.

George Washington 1 ¢ First US President
Palace of the Governors 1 ¼ ¢
A building in Santa Fe, New Mexico that served as
the seat of government of New Mexico for centuries.

Mount Vernon 1 ½ ¢ George Washington's plantation
Thomas Jefferson 2 ¢ Polymath; third US President
Bunker Hill Monument 2 ½ ¢ Battle site of the Revolutionary War
Statue of Liberty 3 ¢ Gifted by the people of France
Abraham Lincoln 4 ¢ 16th US President
Lincoln received a patent for a flotation device that assisted
boats in moving through shallow water.

The Hermitage 4 ½ ¢ Andrew Jackson's plantation
James Monroe 5 ¢ Fifth US President
Theodore Roosevelt 6 ¢ 26th US President
Woodrow Wilson 7 ¢ 28th US President; served during WW1
John J. Pershing 8 ¢ US Army officer during World War I
Alamo 9 ¢ Site of a pivotal Texas Revolution battle
Independence Hall 10 ¢ Independence declared here
Benjamin Harrison 12 ¢ 23rd US President
John Jay 15 ¢ First Chief Justice of the United States
Monticello 20 ¢ Thomas Jefferson's plantation
Paul Revere 25 ¢ Alerted militia of the British approach
Robert E. Lee 30 ¢ Confederate general in the Civil War
John Marshall 40 ¢ Fourth Chief Justice of the US
Susan B. Anthony 50 ¢ Women's suffrage activist
Patrick Henry $1 Leader of the Dec. of Independence
Alexander Hamilton $5 First Secretary of the Treasury

The Biggest Hits When You Were 16

The artists that topped the charts when you turned 16 might not be in your top 10 these days, but you'll probably remember them!

The Troggs 🎸 Wild Thing
Nancy Sinatra 🎸 These Boots Are Made for Walkin'
Frank Sinatra 🎸 Strangers in the Night
The Beatles 🎸 Eleanor Rigby
Percy Sledge 🎸 When a Man Loves a Woman
The Mamas and the Papas 🎸 California Dreamin'
Simon and Garfunkel 🎸 The Sound of Silence
The Young Rascals 🎸 Good Lovin'
The Mindbenders 🎸 A Groovy Kind of Love
The Beatles 🎸 We Can Work It Out
The Four Tops 🎸 Reach Out (I'll Be There)
The Monkees 🎸 Last Train to Clarksville
The Lovin' Spoonful 🎸 Summer in the City
Buck Owens 🎸 Think of Me
The Supremes 🎸 You Can't Hurry Love
Donovan 🎸 Mellow Yellow
Loretta Lynn 🎸 Dear Uncle Sam
The Association 🎸 Cherish
The Rolling Stones 🎸 Paint It Black
Johnny Rivers 🎸 Poor Side of Town
Sonny James 🎸 Take Good Care of Her
The Rolling Stones 🎸 Mother's Little Helper
Wilson Pickett 🎸 Mustang Sally
Ike and Tina Turner 🎸 River Deep, Mountain High

Medical Advances Before You Were 21

A baby born in 1920 USA had a life expectancy of just 55.4 years. By 2000 that was up to 76.8, thanks to medical advances including many of these.

1950	**Polio vaccine** Jonas Salk was asked about taking a patent on the polio vaccine. He replied, "Can you patent the sun?"
1951	Munchhausen syndrome (described)
1954	Kidney transplant
1955	Mass immunization of polio
1956	**Metered-dose inhaler** Invented after the teen daughter of head of Riker Labs asked why her asthma medicine couldn't be in a can like hair spray. At the time, asthma medicine was given in ineffective squeeze bulb glass containers.
1957	EEG topography (toposcope)
1958	Pacemaker
1959	Bone marrow transplant
1960	The pill
1960	Coronary artery bypass surgery
1962	Hip replacement
1962	Beta blocker
1962	First oral polio vaccine (Sabin)
1963	Liver and lung transplants
1963	Valium
1963	Artificial heart
1964	Measles vaccine
1965	Portable defibrillator
1965	Commercial ultrasound
1966	Pancreas transplant
1967	Mumps vaccine
1967	Heart transplant
1968	Powered prosthesis
1968	Controlled drug delivery
1969	Balloon catheter

Blockbuster Movies When You Were 16

These are the movies that everyone was talking about. How many of them did you see (or have you seen since)?

The Blue Max George Peppard, James Mason, Ursula Andress
Peppard learned to fly for the film.

The Sand Pebbles Steve McQueen, Richard Attenborough

The Silencers Dean Martin, Stella Stevens, Daliah Lavi,

Fantastic Voyage Stephen Boyd, Raquel Welch, Edmond O'Brien

Our Man Flint James Coburn, Lee J. Cobb, Gila Golan

Grand Prix James Garner, Eva Marie Saint, Yves Montand

Paradise, Hawaiian Style Elvis Presley, Suzanna Leigh, James Shigeta

The Bible Michael Parks, Ulla Bergryd, Richard Harris

Alfie Michael Caine, Millicent Martin, Julia Foster

Hawaii Julie Andrews, Max von Sydow, Richard Harris

The Professionals Burt Lancaster, Lee Marvin, Robert Ryan

Walk Don't Run Cary Grant, Samantha Eggar, Jim Hutton

Follow Me Boys Fred MacMurray, Vera Miles, Lillian Gish

Lt. Robin Crusoe, U.S.N. Walt Disney, Don DaGradi, Bill Walsh

The Wild Angels Peter Fonda, Nancy Sinatra, Bruce Dern

The Group Candice Bergen, Joan Hackett, Elizabeth Hartman

Georgy Girl Margaret Forster, Peter Nichols, Lynn Redgrave

The Russians Are Coming,
the Russians Are Coming Carl Reiner, Eva Marie Saint, Alan Arkin

Harper Paul Newman, Lauren Bacall, Julie Harris
In the film, Newman dunks his head into ice water, which he did in real life every morning.

The Fortune Cookie Jack Lemmon, Walter Matthau, Ron Rich

A Man for All Seasons Wendy Hiller, Robert Shaw, Orson welles

Who's Afraid of
Virginia Woolf? Elizabeth Taylor, Richard Burton, Sandy Dennis

Torn Curtain Paul Newman, Julie Andrews, Lila Kedrova

Game Show Hosts of the Fifties and Sixties

Many of these men were semi-permanent fixtures, their voices and catchphrases ringing through the decades. Some were full-time entertainers; others were on sabbatical from more serious news duties.

John Charles Daly ➤◄ What's My Line (1950–67)

Art Linkletter ➤◄ People Are Funny (1943–60)

Garry Moore ➤◄ I've Got A Secret (1956–64)

Groucho Marx ➤◄ You Bet Your Life (1949–61)

Warren Hull ➤◄ Strike It Rich (1947–58)

Herb Shriner ➤◄ Two For The Money (1952–56)

George DeWitt ➤◄ Name That Tune (1953–59)

Robert Q. Lewis ➤◄ Name's The Same (1951–54)

Bill Cullen ➤◄ The Price Is Right (1956–65)

Walter Cronkite ➤◄ It's News To Me (1954)
"The most trusted man in America" was briefly the host of this topical quiz game. He didn't do it again.

Bill Slater ➤◄ 20 Questions (1949–52)

Walter Kiernan ➤◄ Who Said That (1951–54)

Bob Eubanks ➤◄ The Newlywed Game (1966–74)

Bud Collyer ➤◄ To Tell The Truth (1956–69)

Jack Barry ➤◄ Twenty-One (1956–58)

Bert Parks ➤◄ Break The Bank (1945–57)

Hugh Downs ➤◄ Concentration (1958–69)

Mike Stokey ➤◄ Pantomime Quiz (1947–59)

Allen Ludden ➤◄ Password (1961–75)

Bob Barker ➤◄ Truth or Consequences (1956–74)
Barker also spent 35 years hosting The Price Is Right.

Hal March ➤◄ $64,000 Question (1955–58)

Monty Hall ➤◄ Let's Make A Deal (1963–91)
Monty—born "Monte", but misspelled on an early publicity photo—was also a philanthropist who raised around $1 billion over his lifetime.

Johnny Carson ➤◄ Who Do You Trust? (1957–63)

Kitchen Inventions

The 20th-century kitchen was a playground for food scientists and engineers with new labor-saving devices and culinary shortcuts launched every year. These all made their debut before you were 18.

1950	Green Garbage Bags
1951	Kenwood food mixer
1952	Automatic coffee pot
1952	Bread clip
1953	Combination washer-dryer
1954	Zipper storage bag
1955	Lint roller
1956	Saran wrap
1957	Homemaker tableware
1958	Rice-a-Roni
1959	Chocolate Velvet Cake invented
1960	**Automated dishwasher**

Electric dishwashers debuted in 1929 but to little acclaim, due in part to the Great Depression and WWII. Automated models with a drying element finally became popular in the 1970s.

1961	Mrs. Butterworth's syrup
1962	Chimney starter
1963	**Veg-O-Matic**

The Veg-O-Matic has increased the cultural lexicon in a number of ways, including "As Seen On TV" and "It slices and dices."

1964	Pop Tarts
1965	Bounty paper towels
1966	Cool Whip
1967	Countertop microwave

Around the World When You Turned 18

These are the headlines from around the globe as you were catapulted into adulthood.

✦ Liberal reforms in Czechoslovakia temporarily result in the Prague Spring
✦ Soviets and allies crush Czechoslovakia
✦ Polish authorities brutally squash student marches
✦ Vietnam War protests occur worldwide
✦ Winter Olympics open in France
✦ Soviet module orbits moon, returns successfully
✦ Businessman buys London Bridge
✦ Pope Paul VI bans Catholics from using birth control pill
✦ Earthquake rocks Sicily
✦ Equatorial Guinea gains independence
✦ Hong Kong flu pandemic kills 1 million worldwide
✦ Students protest in Mexico City
✦ Aswan Dam is completed in Egypt
✦ Protestors in Brazil march against military dictatorship
✦ Volcano in Costa Rica erupts after centuries of dormancy
✦ Australian prime minister disappears
✦ Ferry sinks in New Zealand
✦ Olympics open in Mexico City
✦ Buenos Aires football riot kills 74
✦ Workers and students riot in Paris
✦ Earthquake and tsunami hit the Philippines
✦ English yachtsman sails around the world in 354 days
✦ China celebrates 20 years of rule under Mao
✦ Canada elects Pierre Trudeau as PM
✦ Revolution ends in Peru

Super Bowl Champions Since You Were Born

These are the teams that have held a 7-pound, sterling silver Vince Lombardi trophy aloft during the Super Bowl era, and the number of times they've done it in your lifetime.

- **New England Patriots (6)**
  2001: The Super Bowl MVP, Tom Brady, had been a 6th round draft pick in 2000.
- Pittsburgh Steelers (6)
- Dallas Cowboys (5)
- San Francisco 49ers (5)
- **Green Bay Packers (4)**
  1967: To gain a berth in the Super Bowl, the Packers defeated the Dallas Cowboys in The Ice Bowl at 15 degrees below zero.
- New York Giants (4)
- **Denver Broncos (3)**
  2015: After the Broncos won their first Super Bowl 18 years prior, Broncos owner Pat Bowlen dedicated the victory to long-time quarterback John Elway ("This one's for John!"). After the 2015 victory, John Elway (now general manager) dedicated it to the ailing Bowlen ("This one's for Pat!").
- Washington Football Team (3)
- Las Vegas Raiders (3)
- Miami Dolphins (2)
- Indianapolis Colts (2)
- Kansas City Chiefs (2)
- Baltimore Ravens (2)
- Tampa Bay Buccaneers (2)
- **St. Louis/Los Angeles Rams (2)**
  1999: The Rams were led to the Super Bowl by Kurt Warner, who had been a grocery store clerk after college.
- Seattle Seahawks (1)
- Philadelphia Eagles (1)
- **Chicago Bears (1)**
  The 1985 Bears are known for their song, The Super Bowl Shuffle.
- New York Jets (1)
- New Orleans Saints (1)

Across the Nation

Voting. Joining the military. Turning 18 is serious stuff. Here's what everyone was reading about in the year you reached this milestone.

+ Martin Luther King Jr. assassinated
+ Presidential candidate Bobby Kennedy murdered
+ Richard Nixon elected president
+ Oil beneath Prudhoe Bay discovered
+ Fair Housing Act signed
+ Anti-war protestors occupy Columbus University
+ Special Olympics begin
+ Protestors surround Democrat National Convention
+ Arthur Ashe wins US Open
+ 747 airplane rolls out
+ Manned spacecraft orbits moon and returns safely
+ Two athletes make Black Power salutes
+ Troops commit massacre in Vietnam
+ Swimmer Debbie Meyer wins 3 Olympic gold medals
+ North Korea captures USS Pueblo
+ Tet Offensive occurs in Vietnam
+ President Johnson announces he will not run again
+ Intel Corporation founded
+ Feminists protest Miss America contest
+ Detroit Tigers win World Series
+ Green Bay Packers win Super Bowl again
+ London Bridge bought
+ Redwood National Park established
+ Zodiac killer terrorizes California

Born this year:
- Singer Lisa Marie Presley (right)
- Actor Will Smith
- Actor Terry Crews

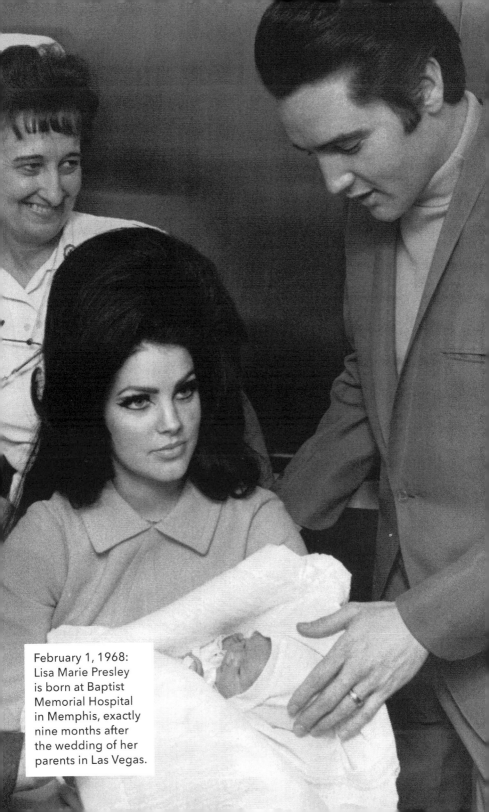

February 1, 1968: Lisa Marie Presley is born at Baptist Memorial Hospital in Memphis, exactly nine months after the wedding of her parents in Las Vegas.

US Open Champions

Winners while you were between the ages of the youngest (John McDermott, 1911, 19 years) and the oldest (Hale Irwin, 1990, at 45). Planning a win? Better hurry up!

1969	Orville Moody
1970	Tony Jacklin
1971	Lee Trevino
1972	Jack Nicklaus
1973	**Johnny Miller**

In 1973, 61-year-old Sam Snead became the oldest player ever to make the cut.

1974	Hale Irwin
1975	Lou Graham
1976	Jerry Pate
1977	Hubert Green
1978	Andy North
1979	Hale Irwin
1980	**Jack Nicklaus**

Nicklaus set the record for years (18) between the first and last US Open victory.

1981	David Graham
1982	Tom Watson
1983	Larry Nelson
1984	Fuzzy Zoeller
1985	Andy North
1986	Raymond Floyd
1987	Scott Simpson
1988	Curtis Strange
1989	Curtis Strange
1990	Hale Irwin
1991	Payne Stewart
1992	Tom Kite
1993	Lee Janzen
1994	Ernie Els
1995	Corey Pavin

Popular Girls' Names

If you started a family at a young age, these are the names you're most likely to have chosen. And even if you didn't pick them, a lot of Americans did!

Jennifer
Having entered theTop 100 in 1956, Jennifer rose rapidly in popularity and in 1970 claimed the top spot where she'd stay for a solid 15 years.

Lisa
Kimberly
Michelle
Amy
Angela
Melissa
Tammy
Mary
Tracy
Julie
Karen
Laura
Christine
Susan
Dawn
Stephanie
Elizabeth
Heather
Kelly
Tina
Shannon
Lori
Patricia
Cynthia

Rising and falling stars:
Tara, Jessica, Tiffany and Traci graced the Top 100 for the first time; for Kim, Carolyn, Carla and Janet it would be their last ever year in the spotlight.

Animals Extinct in Your Lifetime

Billions of passenger pigeons once flew the US skies. By 1914, they had been trapped to extinction. Not every species dies at our hands, but it's a sobering roll-call. (Date is year last known alive or declared extinct).

1951	Yemen gazelle
1952	**Deepwater cisco fish** The deepwater cisco, once found in Lake Huron and Michigan, was overfished and crowded out by invasive parasites and alewife herring. Result? Extinction.
1952	San Benedicto rock wren
1960	Candango mouse, Brasilia
1962	Red-bellied opossum, Argentina
1963	Kākāwahie honeycreeper, Hawaii
1964	South Island snipe, New Zealand
1966	Arabian ostrich
1967	Saint Helena earwig
1967	**Yellow blossom pearly mussel** Habitat loss and pollution proved terminal for this Tennessee resident.
1971	Lake Pedder earthworm, Tasmania
1972	Bushwren, New Zealand
1977	Siamese flat-barbelled catfish, Thailand
1979	Yunnan Lake newt, China
1981	Southern gastric-brooding frog, Australia
1986	Las Vegas dace
1989	Golden toad (see right)
1990	Dusky seaside sparrow, East Coast USA
2000	**Pyrenean ibex, Iberia** For a few minutes in 2003 this species was brought back to life through cloning, but sadly the newborn female ibex died.
2001	Caspian tiger, Central Asia
2008	Saudi gazelle
2012	**Pinta giant tortoise** The rarest creature in the world for the latter half of his 100-year life, Lonesome George of the Galapagos was the last remaining Pinta tortoise.

The observed history of the golden toad is brief and tragic. It wasn't discovered until 1964, abundant in a pristine area of Costa Rica. By 1989 it had gone, a victim of rising temperatures.

Popular Boys' Names

Here are the top boys' names for this year. Many of the most popular choices haven't shifted much since you were born, but more modern names are creeping in…

Michael

For 44 years from 1954 onwards, Michael was the nation's most popular name. (There was one blip in 1960 when David came first.)

James
David
John
Robert
Christopher
William
Brian
Mark
Richard
Jeffrey
Scott
Jason
Kevin
Steven
Joseph
Thomas
Eric
Daniel
Timothy
Charles
Anthony
Paul
Matthew
Kenneth
Gregory
Stephen

Rising and falling stars:

A healthy crop of new names this year: Travis, Jeremy, Adam, Marcus, Lance, Derek, Derrick, Juan and Carlos. Martin, Bruce, Jay and Randall leave us.

Popular Movies When You Were 21

The biggest stars in the biggest movies: these are the films the nation were enjoying as you entered into adulthood.

The Big Doll House 🎬 Pam Grier, Judy Brown, Roberta Collins
Play Misty for Me 🎬 Clint Eastwood, Jessica Walter, Donna Mills
Fiddler on the Roof 🎬 Topol, Norma Crane, Leonard Frey
The Last Picture Show 🎬 Timothy Bottoms, Jeff Bridges, Ellen Burstyn
Willard 🎬 Bruce Davison, Ernest Borgnine, Sondra Locke
Bedknobs and Broomsticks 🎬 Angela Lansbury, David Tomlinson, John Ericson
Dirty Harry 🎬 Clint Eastwood, Andy Robinson, Harry Guardino
The Hospital 🎬 George C. Scott, Diana Rigg, Barnard Hughes
Shaft 🎬 Richard Roundtree, Moses Gunn, Charles Cioffi
In Ernest Tidyman's novels, the Shaft character was white.
The French Connection 🎬 Gene Hackman, Fernando Rey, Roy Scheider
Willy Wonka & the Chocolate Factory 🎬 Gene Wilder, Jack Albertson, Peter Ostrum
Billy Jack 🎬 Tom Laughlin, Delores Taylor, David Roya
Carnal Knowledge 🎬 Jack Nicholson, Art Garfunkel, Ann-Margret
Big Jake 🎬 John Wayne, Richard Boone, Maureen O'Hara
A Clockwork Orange 🎬 Malcolm McDowell, Patrick Magee, Adrienne Corri
Macbeth 🎬 Jon Finch, Francesca Annis, Martin Shaw
Tuesday Weld Rejected the role due to nudity in the script.
Klute 🎬 Jane Fonda, Donald Sutherland, Charles Cioffi
Diamonds Are Forever 🎬 Sean Connery, Jill St. John, Charles Gray
The Andromeda Strain 🎬 Arthur Hill, James Olson, Kate Reid
Summer of '42 🎬 Jennifer O'Neill, Gary Grimes, Jerry Houser
Cold Turkey 🎬 Dick Van Dyke, Pippa Scott, Tom Poston
Sweet Sweetback's Baad Asssss Song 🎬 Melvin Van Peebles, Hubert Scales
Escape from the Planet of the Apes 🎬 Roddy McDowall, Kim Hunter, Bradford Dillman
McCabe & Mrs. Miller 🎬 Warren Beatty, Julie Christie, Rene Auberjonois

Across the Nation

A selection of national headlines from the year you turned 21. But how many can you remember?

- Walt Disney World opens in Florida
- Commercial whale hunting ends
- Uniform Monday Holiday Act takes effect
- Baltimore Colts win the Super Bowl
- Earthquake hits Los Angeles area, kills 64
- Satchel Paige voted into Baseball Hall of Fame
- Tornadoes hit Mississippi Delta region
- Bomb explodes in US Capitol Building
- Starbucks begins serving coffee
- Supreme Court finds for busing students to desegregate schools
- Trade embargo with China lifted
- Southwest Airlines begins flying
- Post Office Department replaced by the US Postal Service
- John F. Kennedy Center for the Performing Arts opens
- Attica Prison riots erupt
- Pittsburgh Pirates wins the World Series
- D.B. Cooper parachutes after hijacking airliner (right)
- Political Libertarian party founded
- Pentagon Papers published
- Amtrak replaces private operators, halving train services
- "Ping Pong Diplomacy" begins
- Federal Express starts shipping
- Dollar no longer backed by gold or silver
- Floppy disks invented

Born this year:
- Businessman Elon Musk
- Actress Winona Ryder
- Rapper Tupac Shakur

Robert Lee Jackson steps off the aircraft he and his girlfriend had hijacked near Texas, forcing it to fly on to Mexico, Peru, and its final stop in Argentina—a record hijack distance of 7,700 miles. The $100,000 ransom he had extracted was recovered.

The same cannot be said of the $200,000 bagged by "D.B. Cooper," a mysterious hijacker who had requested parachutes. Over Nevada, in the middle of a storm, the man opened the door and jumped. Barring a small bundle of banknotes found in 1980, neither he nor the money were ever seen again.

The Biggest Hits When You Were 21

The artists you love at 21 are with you for life. How many of these hits from this milestone year can you still hum or sing in the tub?

George Harrison 🎵 My Sweet Lord
Rod Stewart 🎵 Maggie May
Tom Jones 🎵 She's a Lady
Carole King 🎵 It's Too Late
The Rolling Stones 🎵 Brown Sugar
John Lennon 🎵 Imagine
Janis Joplin 🎵 Me and Bobby McGee
Marvin Gaye 🎵 What's Going On
Dolly Parton 🎵 Joshua
Elton John 🎵 Your Song
Ringo Starr 🎵 It Don't Come Easy
The Temptations 🎵 Just My Imagination
(Running Away with Me)
Sammi Smith 🎵 Help Me Make It
Through the Night
Al Green 🎵 Let's Stay Together
The Jackson 5 🎵 Never Can Say Goodbye
Stevie Wonder 🎵 If You Really Love Me
King Floyd 🎵 Groove Me
Creedence Clearwater Revival 🎵 Who'll Stop the Rain
Johnny Cash 🎵 Man in Black
Sly and the Family Stone 🎵 Family Affair
The Beatles 🎵 Let It Be
George Jones 🎵 A Good Year for the Roses
Jean Knight 🎵 Mr. Big Stuff
Van Morrison 🎵 Blue Money

Popular Food in the 1960s

Changes in society didn't stop at the front door: a revolution in the kitchen brought us exotic new recipes, convenience in a can, and even space-age fruit flavors. These are the tastes of a decade, but how many of them were on the menu for your family?

McDonald's Big Mac
First served in 1967 by a Pittsburgh franchisee.
Royal Shake-a-Pudd'n Dessert Mix
Tunnel of Fudge Cake
Campbell's SpaghettiOs
Pop-Tarts
B&M's canned bread

Cool Whip
A time-saving delight that originally contained no milk or cream, meaning that it could be frozen and transported easily.

Grasshopper pie
Beech-Nut Fruit Stripe Gum
Sandwich Loaf

Lipton Onion Soup Dip
Millions of packets are still sold each year of this favorite that was once known as "Californian Dip".

Jello salad
Hires Root Beer
Baked Alaska

Tang
Invented by William A. Mitchell who also concocted Cool Whip, Tang was used by astronauts to flavor the otherwise unpalatable water on board the Gemini and Apollo missions.

Corn Diggers
Teem soda
Eggo Waffles
Kraft Shake 'N Bake

Maypo oatmeal
In 1985, Dire Straights sang, "I want my MTV"—an echo of the stars who'd shouted the same words to promote the new station. But 30 years before that (and the inspiration for MTV's campaign), an animated child yelled, "I want my Maypo!"

Fashion in the Sixties

As a child, you (generally) wear what you're given. It's only in hindsight, on fading Polaroids, that you recognize that your outfits carried the fashion imprint of the day. Whether you were old or bold enough to carry off a pair of bell bottoms, though, is a secret that should remain between you and your photo albums.

Bell bottoms
Bell bottoms were widely available at Navy surplus and thrift stores at a time when second-hand shopping was on the rise.

Miniskirts and mini dresses

Peasant blouses

Rudi Gernreich
Pope Paul IV banned Catholics from wearing his monokini—a topless swim suit.

US flag clothing

Tulle turbans

Shift dresses

Collarless jackets
This jacket trend was popularized by the Beatles in 1963.

Babydoll dresses

V-neck tennis sweaters

Afghan coats

Leopard print clothing
In 1962, Jackie Kennedy wore a leopard print coat which caused a spike in demand for leopard skin, leading to the death of up to 250,000 leopards. The coat's designer, Oleg Cassini, felt guilty about it for the rest of his life.

Tie-dye clothing

Short, brightly colored, shapeless dresses

Pillbox hats

Mary Quant

Maxi skirts

Bonnie Cashin

Plaid

Poor boy sweaters

Pea coats

Around the World When You Turned 25

With the growing reach of news organizations, events from outside our borders were sometimes front-page news. How many do you remember?

+ Spanish dictator Franco dies
+ Khmer Rouge genocide begins
+ OPEC raises price for oil by 10%
+ Chinese dams fail
+ Attacker slashes the painting "The Night Watch"
+ Saudi king is murdered by nephew
+ UK Conservative Party chooses Thatcher to lead it
+ VHS and Betamax machines go on sale in Japan
+ International Year of the Woman is declared by UN
+ IRA commits more murder and terror in London
+ Angola civil war begins
+ Lebanon civil war begins
+ Suriname gains independence
+ Suez Canal reopens after being closed during Six-Day War
+ Mozambique gains independence
+ Over 350,000 Moroccans make the "Green March"
+ Terrorists attack West German embassy in Stockholm
+ Coup overthrows Chad government
+ Woman conquers Everest
+ Queen knights Charlie Chaplin
+ East Timor declares its independence
+ Dutch Elm disease decimates UK elm trees
+ India PM found guilty of corruption
+ Earthquake strike China
+ Spain abandons Western Sahara

Cars of the 1960s

Smaller cars. More powerful cars. More distinctive cars. More variety, yes: but the success of imported models such as the Volkswagen Beetle was a sign that more fundamental changes lay ahead for The Big Three.

1940	Ford Lincoln Continental
1949	Volkswagen Beetle
1950	Volkswagen Type 2 (Microbus)
1958	**General Motors Chevrolet Impala** In 1965, the Impala sold more than 1 million units, the most sold by any model in the US since WWII.
1958	American Motors Corporation Rambler Ambassador
1959	General Motors Chevrolet El Camino
1959	Ford Galaxie
1960	**Ford Falcon** The cartoon strip "Peanuts" was animated for TV to market the Falcon.
1960	General Motors Pontiac Tempest
1960	General Motors Chevrolet Corvair
1961	**Jaguar E-Type** Ranked first in The Daily Telegraph UK's list of the world's "100 most beautiful cars" of all time.
1961	Chrysler Newport
1962	Shelby Cobra
1963	General Motors Buick Riviera
1963	Porsche 911
1963	Kaiser-Jeep Jeep Wagoneer
1964	**Ford Mustang** The song of the same name reached #6 on the R&B Charts in 1966. That year, more Ford Mustangs were sold (550,000) than any other car.
1964	General Motors Chevrolet Chevelle
1964	Chrysler Plymouth Barracuda
1964	General Motors Pontiac GTO
1967	General Motors Chevrolet Camaro
1967	Ford Mercury Cougar
1968	Chrysler Plymouth Road Runner

Books of the Decade

Were you a voracious bookworm in your twenties? Or a more reluctant reader, only drawn by the biggest titles of the day? Here are the new titles that fought for your attention.

1970	Love Story by Erich Segal
1970	One Hundred Years of Solitude by Gabriel Garcia Marquez
1971	The Happy Hooker: My Own Story by Xaviera Hollander
1971	The Exorcist by William Peter Blatty
1972	Watership Down by Richard Adams
1972	The Joy of Sex by Alex Comfort
1972	Fear and Loathing in Las Vegas by Hunter S. Thompson
1973	Fear of Flying by Erica Jong
1973	Gravity's Rainbow by Thomas Pynchon
1974	Jaws by Peter Benchley
1974	The Front Runner by Patricia Nell Warren
1975	The Eagle Has Landed by Jack Higgins
1975	Shōgun by James Clavell
1975	Ragtime by E.L. Doctorow
1976	Roots by Alex Haley
1976	The Hite Report by Shere Hite
1977	The Thorn Birds by Colleen McCullough
1977	The Women's Room by Marilyn French
1978	Eye of the Needle by Ken Follett
1978	The World According to Garp by John Irving
1979	Flowers in the Attic by V.C. Andrews
1979	The Hitchhiker's Guide to the Galaxy by Douglas Adams
1979	Sophie's Choice by William Styron

Prominent Americans

This new set of definitive stamps, issued from 1965 onwards, aimed to do a better job of capturing the diversity of the Americans who made a nation. The series doubled the previous number of women depicted...to two. How many did you have in your collection?

Thomas Jefferson 1 ¢ 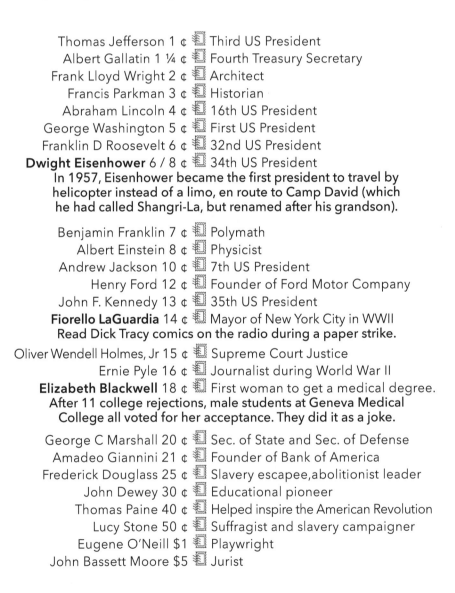 Third US President

Albert Gallatin 1 ¼ ¢ Fourth Treasury Secretary

Frank Lloyd Wright 2 ¢ Architect

Francis Parkman 3 ¢ Historian

Abraham Lincoln 4 ¢ 16th US President

George Washington 5 ¢ First US President

Franklin D Roosevelt 6 ¢ 32nd US President

Dwight Eisenhower 6 / 8 ¢ 34th US President
In 1957, Eisenhower became the first president to travel by helicopter instead of a limo, en route to Camp David (which he had called Shangri-La, but renamed after his grandson).

Benjamin Franklin 7 ¢ Polymath

Albert Einstein 8 ¢ Physicist

Andrew Jackson 10 ¢ 7th US President

Henry Ford 12 ¢ Founder of Ford Motor Company

John F. Kennedy 13 ¢ 35th US President

Fiorello LaGuardia 14 ¢ Mayor of New York City in WWII
Read Dick Tracy comics on the radio during a paper strike.

Oliver Wendell Holmes, Jr 15 ¢ Supreme Court Justice

Ernie Pyle 16 ¢ Journalist during World War II

Elizabeth Blackwell 18 ¢ First woman to get a medical degree.
After 11 college rejections, male students at Geneva Medical College all voted for her acceptance. They did it as a joke.

George C Marshall 20 ¢ Sec. of State and Sec. of Defense

Amadeo Giannini 21 ¢ Founder of Bank of America

Frederick Douglass 25 ¢ Slavery escapee, abolitionist leader

John Dewey 30 ¢ Educational pioneer

Thomas Paine 40 ¢ Helped inspire the American Revolution

Lucy Stone 50 ¢ Suffragist and slavery campaigner

Eugene O'Neill $1 Playwright

John Bassett Moore $5 Jurist

Sixties Game Shows

Recovery from the quiz show scandal of the fifties was a gradual process. Big prize money was out; games were in—the sillier the better, or centered around relationships. "Popcorn for the mind," as game show creator Chuck Barris memorably put it.

College Bowl 🏆 (1953-70)
Snap Judgment 🏆 (1967-69)
To Tell The Truth 🏆 (1956-present)
Dough Re Mi 🏆 (1958-60)
Camouflage 🏆 (1961-62 & 1980)
Dream House 🏆 (1968-84)
Say When!! 🏆 (1961-65)
Let's Make A Deal 🏆 (1963-present)
The long-time presenter of the show, Monty Hall, gave rise to the eponymous problem: when one door in three hides a prize and you've made your pick, should you change your answer when the host reveals a "zonk" (dud) behind another door? (The counterintuitive answer is yes!)

Your First Impression 🏆 (1962-64)
Supermarket Sweep 🏆 (1965-present)
In one of its many comebacks, 1990 episodes of Supermarket Sweep featured monsters roaming the aisles including Frankenstein and Mr. Yuk.

You Don't Say! 🏆 1963-79)
It's Your Bet 🏆 (1969-73)
Yours For A Song 🏆 (1961-63)
Concentration 🏆 (1958-91)
Seven Keys 🏆 (1960-65)
Queen For A Day 🏆 1945-1970)
Password 🏆 (1961-75)
Video Village 🏆 (1960-62)
Who Do You Trust? 🏆 (1957-63)
Originally titled, "Do You Trust Your Wife?"
Personality 🏆 (1967-69)
Beat The Odds 🏆 (1961-69)

Across the Nation

Another decade passes and you're well into adulthood. Were you reading the news, or making it? Here are the national stories that dominated the front pages.

- ✦ Mount St. Helens erupts
- ✦ CNN begins broadcasting
- ✦ Staggers Act deregulates the rail industry (1st time since 1887)
- ✦ Post-it Notes go on sale
- ✦ Men's hockey team beats Soviets on way to Olympic gold
- ✦ John Lennon shot
- ✦ Fire at MGM Grand Hotel kills 85
- ✦ Rioting in Miami leaves 17 dead
- ✦ Lake Placid hosts Winter Olympics
- ✦ Ronald Reagan elected president
- ✦ Operation to rescue hostages in Iran fails
- ✦ Boycott of Summer Olympics over Soviet invasion of Afghanistan
- ✦ Cubans flee Cuba in the Mariel Boatlift
- ✦ Far Side cartoon begins publication
- ✦ Big League Chew gum goes on sale
- ✦ All men (18-25 years old) have to sign up for selective service
- ✦ Severe heat wave strikes
- ✦ Philadelphia Phillies win the World Series
- ✦ Super Bowl winners are again the Pittsburgh Steelers
- ✦ Jack Nicklaus takes the US Open
- ✦ John McEnroe and Chris Evert rule the tennis courts
- ✦ Rubik's Cube begins to puzzle people
- ✦ Killer Clown John Wayne Gacy sentenced to death
- ✦ Arthur Ashe retires from tennis

Born this year:
- ⚘ Actor Macaulay Culkin
- ⚘ TV star Kim Kardashian
- ⚘ Actress Christina Ricci
- ⚘ Singer Christina Aguilera

Three days after John Lennon was shot and killed on December 8, 1980, the shock is still written on the face of fans. They're gathered outside the Dakota Building where Mark Chapman calmly waited to be arrested, holding a copy of The Catcher in the Rye. There was no funeral; in its place, Yoko requested ten minutes' silence. And on the following Sunday, every New York radio

The Biggest Hits When You Were 30...

How many of these big tunes from the year you turned thirty will still strike a chord decades later?

John Lennon 🎵 (Just Like) Starting Over
Diana Ross 🎵 Upside Down
Kool & the Gang 🎵 Celebration
Blondie 🎵 Call Me
Devo 🎵 Whip It
Stephanie Mills 🎵 Never Knew Love Like This Before
Michael Jackson 🎵 Rock with You
Pink Floyd 🎵 Another Brick in the Wall (Part 2)
George Benson 🎵 Give Me the Night
Eddie Rabbitt 🎵 Drivin' My Life Away
The Rolling Stones 🎵 Emotional Rescue
The Whispers 🎵 And the Beat Goes On
Willie Nelson 🎵 On the Road Again
Stevie Wonder 🎵 Master Blaster (Jammin')
Billy Joel 🎵 You May Be Right
The S.O.S. Band 🎵 Take Your Time (Do It Right) [Part 1]
Queen 🎵 Another One Bites the Dust
Waylon Jennings 🎵 Theme from The Dukes of Hazzard
(Good Ol' Boys)
Lipps Inc. 🎵 Funkytown
The Manhattans 🎵 Shining Star
AC/DC 🎵 Back in Black
Anne Murray 🎵 Could I Have This Dance
The J. Geils Band 🎵 Love Stinks
Journey 🎵 Any Way You Want It

...and the Movies You Saw That Year, Too

From award winners to crowd pleasers, here are the movies that played as your third decade drew to a close.

The Shining 🎬 Jack Nicholson, Shelley Duvall, Danny Lloyd

The Blue Lagoon 🎬 Brooke Shields, Christopher Atkins, Leo McKern

Star Wars Ep. V: The Empire Strikes Back 🎬 Mark Hamill, Harrison Ford, Carrie Fisher

Flash Gordon 🎬 Sam J. Jones, Melody Anderson, Ornella Muti

Stir Crazy 🎬 Gene Wilder, Richard Pryor

Airplane! 🎬 Robert Hays, Julie Hagerty, Leslie Nielson
Director David Zucker deliberately aimed to cast actors without comedic experience, feeling they would be funnier than comedians.

Mad Max 🎬 Mel Gibson, Joanne Samuel, Hugh Keays-Byrne

The Final Countdown 🎬 Kirk Douglas, Martin Sheen, James Farentino

American Gigolo 🎬 Richard Gere, Lauren Hutton, Bill Duke

Private Benjamin 🎬 Goldie Hawn, Albert Brooks, Eileen Brennan

Brubaker 🎬 Robert Redford, Yaphet Kotto, Jane Alexander

Popeye 🎬 Robin Williams, Shelley Duvall, Paul L. Smith

Any Which Way You Can 🎬 Clint Eastwood, Sondra Locke, Geoffrey Lewis

Caddyshack 🎬 Chevy Chase, Rodney Dangerfield, Ted Knight

The Elephant Man 🎬 John Hurt, Anthony Hopkins, Anne Bancroft

Smokey and the Bandit II 🎬 Burt Reynolds, Sally Field, Jerry Reed

Ordinary People 🎬 Donald Sutherland, Mary Tyler Moore, Judd Hirsch

Urban Cowboy 🎬 John Travolta, Debra Winger, Scott Glenn

Nine to Five 🎬 Jane Fonda, Lily Tomlin, Dolly Parton

Friday the 13th 🎬 Betsy Palmer, Adrienne King, Harry Crosby

The Blues Brothers 🎬 John Belushi, Dan Aykroyd, Cab Calloway
Dan Aykroyd insisted that James Brown, Ray Charles, Aretha Franklin and Cab Calloway were all given speaking roles.

Around the House

Sometimes with a fanfare but often by stealth, inventions and innovations transformed the 20th-century household. Here's what arrived between the ages of 10 and 30.

1961	Head & Shoulders shampoo
1962	Arco lamp
1963	**Chips Ahoy! chocolate chip cookies**

An elementary teacher and her class wrote Nabisco saying that they did not find 1000 chips in the bag of Chips Ahoy, though the bag clearly states it has that many. Nabisco flew a representative to their school and demonstrated to the students (and the media) how to actually find all the chips.

1963	Push button Touchtone phone
1963	Lava lamps
1964	Portable TVs
1964	Sharpie permanent markers
1965	Cordless telephone
1967	Close-up toothpaste
1968	Bean bag chair
1969	Nerf dart guns
1970	**Irish Spring soap**

Irish Spring soap's catchy tune and tag lines became part of the language with "Clean as a whistle" and "I like it too!" While it generated a lot of bad Irish accents, it has nothing to do with Ireland.

1971	Soft contact lenses
1972	Science calculator
1973	BIC lighter
1974	Rubik's Cube
1975	Betamax video tape machine
1976	VHS video tape machine
1978	Cordless drill
1979	**Sony Walkman**

The Walkman was born when the co-founder of Sony wanted an easier way to listen to opera.

Here's one that didn't quite make the grade: AT&T's Picturephone, demonstrated here at the 1964 New York World's Fair. A trial set up that year invited the public to rent two of the Picturephone rooms set up in New York, Chicago, and Washington ($16 for 3 minutes). The take-up over the following years was almost nil, but Picturephones went on sale in 1970 anyway with a prediction of a billion-dollar business by 1980. The devices

Female Olympic Gold Medalists in Your Lifetime

These are the women who have stood atop the podium the greatest number of times at the Summer Olympics, whether in individual or team events.

Jenny Thompson (8) 🥇 Swimming
Thompson is an anesthesiologist. She started her medical training in 2000—although she took time out while studying to win further gold World Championship medals.

Katie Ledecky (7) 🥇 Swimming
Allyson Felix (7) 🥇 Athletics
Amy Van Dyken (6) 🥇 Swimming
Dana Vollmer (5) 🥇 Swimming
Missy Franklin (5) 🥇 Swimming
Sue Bird (5) 🥇 Basketball
Diana Taurasi (5) 🥇 Basketball
The late Kobe Bryant dubbed Taurasi the "white mamba"; for others she is the G.O.A.T. in women's basketball.

Allison Schmitt (4) 🥇 Swimming
Dara Torres (4) 🥇 Swimming
Evelyn Ashford (4) 🥇 Athletics
Janet Evans (4) 🥇 Swimming
Lisa Leslie (4) 🥇 Basketball
Pat McCormick (4) 🥇 Diving
Sanya Richards-Ross (4) 🥇 Athletics
Serena Williams (4) 🥇 Tennis
Simone Biles (4) 🥇 Gymnastics
Biles's phenomenal medal tally in Olympics and World Championships is greater than any other US gymnast.

Tamika Catchings (4) 🥇 Basketball
Teresa Edwards (4) 🥇 Basketball
Venus Williams (4) 🥇 Tennis

Around the World When You Turned 35

It's a big news day every day, somewhere in the world. Here are the stories that the media thought you'd want to read in the year of your 35th birthday.

- ✦ Live Aid concerts held for famine relief
- ✦ French agents sink Greenpeace ship
- ✦ Gorbachev becomes Soviet leader
- ✦ Japan selects three astronauts
- ✦ Earthquake registers 8.1 in Mexico City
- ✦ Rioting breaks out in UK cities
- ✦ Boris Becker wins Wimbledon
- ✦ Police clash with demonstrators at Stonehenge
- ✦ Israel airlifts thousands of Jewish refugees from Sudan
- ✦ Colombian volcano erupts, killing around 25,000
- ✦ Terrorists hijack Achille Lauro
- ✦ Rome and Vienna airports are attacked by terrorists
- ✦ Brussels stadium hooliganism kills 39 as wall collapses
- ✦ South Africa invades Angola
- ✦ Massive car bomb explodes in Beirut
- ✦ Riots continue in South Africa against apartheid
- ✦ Switzerland passes law requiring catalytic converters on private cars
- ✦ UK scientists discover hole in ozone
- ✦ Train disaster in Ethiopia leaves over 400 dead
- ✦ Female math prodigy graduates from Oxford at 13 years old
- ✦ South Korea opens the tallest building outside North America
- ✦ Japan Air crash kills 520—worst single-aircraft disaster
- ✦ Kuwait gives voting rights to women
- ✦ Egyptian airliner is hijacked
- ✦ Cities in Nepal are targets of bomb attacks

Drinks of the Sixties

For many of those slipping from adolescence into adulthood, your choice of drink says a lot about you. Sophisticated or down-to-earth? A classic, or something to make a statement? In the years that follow, the drinks might change, but the decision remains the same! Here's what was behind a sixties bar.

Falstaff beer
Rusty Nail cocktail
Rumored to be a favorite drink of the Rat Pack.

Hull's Cream Ale
Stinger cocktail
Rheingold Extra Dry Lager
Gunther's Beer
Lone Star Beer
The Gimlet cocktail
The Grasshopper cocktail
Little King's Cream Ale
Best known for its miniature seven-ounce bottles.

Mai Thai cocktail
Genesee Cream Ale
Storz Beer
From Nebraska, Storz was "Brewed for the beer pro."

Iron City Beer
Iron City is reputed to have introduced the first twist-off bottle cap in 1963.

Golden Dream cocktail
Mint Julep cocktail
It's the official drink of the Kentucky Derby, with around 120,000 served over the weekend.

Koch's Light Lager Beer
Arrow 77 Beer
Daiquiri cocktail
Manhattan cocktail
Sterling Premium Pilsner
Carling Black Label
Hamm's Beer
Old fashioned cocktail

Seventies Game Shows

With enough water under the bridge since the 1950s scandals, producers of seventies game shows injected big money into new formats and revamped favorites, some of them screened five nights a week. How many did you cheer on from the couch?

High Rollers 🏆 (1974–88)

Gambit 🏆 (1972–81)

The New Treasure Hunt 🏆 (1973–82)
Perhaps the best-known episode of this show saw a woman faint when she won a Rolls Royce–that she later had to sell in order to pay the taxes.

The Cross-Wits 🏆 (1975–87)

Hollywood Squares 🏆 1966–2004)

The Newlywed Game 🏆 (1966–2013)
Show creator Chuck Barris also made "3's a Crowd"– the show in which men, their secretaries and their wives competed. The public wasn't happy.

Pyramid 🏆 (1973–present)
Thanks to inflation and rival prizes, the $10,000 Pyramid in 1973 didn't last long: from 1976 it was raised in increments to its current peak of $100,000.

Dealer's Choice 🏆 (1974–75)

Sports Challenge 🏆 (1971–79)

Tattletales 🏆 (1974–84)

It's Your Bet 🏆 (1969–73)

Celebrity Sweepstakes 🏆 (1974–77)

Rhyme and Reason 🏆 (1975–76)

Three On A Match 🏆 (1971–74)

The Match Game 🏆 (1962–present)

Sale of the Century 🏆 (1969–89)

The Dating Game 🏆 (1965–99)
The Dating Game–known as Blind Date in many international versions–saw many celebrity appearances before they became well-known, including the Carpenters and Arnold Schwarzenegger.

Popular Boys' Names

40

Just as middle age crept up unnoticed, so the most popular names also evolved. The traditional choices—possibly including yours—are fast losing their appeal to new parents.

Michael
Christopher
Matthew
For fourteen years from 1980, tastes in baby names were locked tight at the top: Michael was the most popular, Christopher was runner-up with Matthew in third spot.

Joshua
Daniel
David
Andrew
James
Justin
Joseph
Ryan
John
Robert
Nicholas
Anthony
William
Jonathan
Kyle
Brandon
Jacob
Tyler
Zachary
Kevin
Eric
Steven
Thomas

Rising and falling stars:
New entries were Dylan, Jesus, Garrett and Miguel; Chad, Donald and Ronald all took their leave.

Popular Girls' Names

It's a similar story for girls' names. Increasing numbers are taking their infant inspiration from popular culture. The worlds of music, film and theater are all fertile hunting grounds for those in need of inspiration.

Jessica
Ashley
Brittany
Amanda
Samantha
Sarah
Stephanie
Jennifer
Elizabeth
A name's moment in the sun spans years, sometimes decades. But eventually they disappear out of sight... unless you're Elizabeth. For over a century she's floated between 6th and 26th position.

Lauren
Megan
Emily
Nicole
Kayla
Amber
Rachel
Courtney
Danielle
Heather
Melissa
Rebecca
Michelle
Tiffany
Chelsea
Rising and falling stars:
Girls we welcomed for the first time this year: Olivia, Paige, Ariel, Alexandria, Gabrielle and Shelby. Names we'd never see in the Top 100 again: Tara, Kathleen and Patricia.

NBA Champions
Since You Were Born

These are the winners of the NBA Finals in your lifetime—
and the number of times they've taken the title.

- ⦿ Philadelphia Warriors (1)
- ⦿ Minneapolis Lakers (4)
- ⦿ Rochester Royals (1)
- ⦿ Syracuse Nationals (1)
- ⦿ **Boston Celtics (17)**
  1966: After the Lakers won Game 1 of the NBA Finals, the Celtics named their star Bill Russell player-coach. He was the first black coach in the NBA. The Celtics responded by winning the series.

- ⦿ St. Louis Hawks (1)
- ⦿ Philadelphia 76ers (2)
- ⦿ New York Knicks (2)
- ⦿ Milwaukee Bucks (2)
- ⦿ **Los Angeles Lakers (12)**
  1980: With Kareem Abdul-Jabbar out with an injury, Lakers' 20-year-old rookie Magic Johnson started at center in the clinching Game 6 and scored 42 points and snared 15 rebounds.

- ⦿ **Golden State Warriors (4)**
  2015: LeBron James and Stephen Curry, the stars of the teams that faced off in the 2015 NBA Finals, were both born in the same hospital in Akron, Ohio.

- ⦿ Portland Trail Blazers (1)
- ⦿ Washington Bullets (1)
- ⦿ Seattle SuperSonics (1)
- ⦿ Detroit Pistons (3)
- ⦿ Chicago Bulls (6)
- ⦿ Houston Rockets (2)
- ⦿ San Antonio Spurs (5)
- ⦿ Miami Heat (3)
- ⦿ Dallas Mavericks (1)
- ⦿ Cleveland Cavaliers (1)
- ⦿ Toronto Raptors (1)

Fashion in the Seventies

The decade that taste forgot? Or a kickback against the sixties and an explosion of individuality? Skirts got shorter (and longer). Block colors and peasant chic vied with sequins and disco glamor. How many of your seventies outfits would you still wear today?

Wrap dresses
Diane von Fürstenberg said she invented the silent, no-zipper wrap dress for one-night stands. "Haven't you ever tried to creep out of the room unnoticed the following morning? I've done that many times."

Tube tops
Midi skirt
In 1970, fashion designers began to lower the hemlines on the mini skirt. This change wasn't welcomed by many consumers. Women picketed in New York City with "stop the midi" signs.

Track suit, running shoes, soccer jerseys
Cowl neck sweaters
His & hers matching outfits
Cork-soled platform shoes
Caftans, Kaftans, Kimonos and mummus
Prairie dresses
Cuban heels
Gaucho pants
Chokers and dog collars as necklaces
Birkenstocks
Tennis headbands
Turtleneck shirts
Puffer vests
Long knit vests layered over tops and pants
Military surplus rucksack bags
"Daisy Dukes" denim shorts
Daisy's revealing cut-off denim shorts in The Dukes of Hazzard caught the attention of network censors. The answer for actor Catherine Bach? Wear flesh-colored pantyhose—just in case.

Yves Saint Laurent
Shrink tops
Bill Gibb

Drinks of the Seventies

Breweries were bigger, and there were fewer of them. Beers were lighter. But what could you (or your parents) serve with your seventies fondue? How about a cocktail that's as heavy on the double-entendre as it was on the sloe gin? Or perhaps match the decade's disco theme with a splash of blue curaçao?

Amber Moon cocktail
Features an unbroken, raw egg and featured in the film Murder on the Orient Express.

Billy Beer
Rainier Beer
Point Special Lager
Tequila Sunrise cocktail
Regal Select Light Beer
Stroh's rum
Long Island Iced Tea cocktail
Merry Widow cocktail
Shell's City Pilsner Premium Beer
Brass Monkey cocktail
The Godfather cocktail
Brown Derby
Sea-Breeze cocktail

Schlitz
This Milwaukee brewery was the country's largest in the late sixties and early seventies. But production problems were followed by a disastrous ad campaign, and by 1981 the original brewery was closed.

Alabama Slammer cocktail
Golden Cadillac cocktail
Harvey Wallbanger cocktail
Red White & Blue Special Lager Beer
Lite Beer from Miller

Coors Banquet Beer
A beer that made the most of its initial limited distribution network by floating the idea of contraband Coors. The idea was so successful that Coors smuggling became central to the plot of the movie Smokey and the Bandit.

US Open Tennis

Across the Open Era and the US National Championship that preceded it, these men won between the year you turned 19 (matching the youngest ever champ, Pete Sampras) and 38 (William Larned's age with his seventh win, in 1911).

1969	Rod Laver
1970	Ken Rosewall
1971	Stan Smith
1972	Illie Nastase
1973	John Newcombe
1974	Jimmy Connors
1975	**Manuel Orantes**

Orantes came back from 5-0 down in the 4th set of the semifinal to win the 4th and 5th sets and upset top-seeded Jimmy Connors in the final.

1976	Jimmy Connors
1977	Guillermo Vilas
1978	**Jimmy Connors**

Connors became the only player to win on all three surfaces that have been used by the US Open.

1979-81	John McEnroe
1982-83	Jimmy Connors
1984	John McEnroe
1985-87	Ivan Lendl

Lendl was the world's number 1 player for 270 weeks during the eighties, though a win at Wimbledon eluded him. His low-key persona earned him the cutting Sports Illustrated headline, "The Champion That Nobody Cares About".

1988	Mats Wilander

Books of the Decade

Family, friends, TV, and more: there are as many midlife distractions as there are books on the shelf. Did you get drawn in by these bestsellers, all published in your thirties?

1980	Rage of Angels by Sidney Sheldon
1980	The Bourne Identity by Robert Ludlum
1980	The Covenant by James Michener
1981	The Hotel New Hampshire by John Irving
1981	Noble House by James Clavell
1981	An Indecent Obsession by Colleen McCullough
1982	The Color Purple by Alice Walker
1982	Space by James A. Michener
1983	Pet Sematary by Stephen King
1983	Hollywood Wives by Jackie Collins
1984	You Can Heal Your Life by Louise Hay
1984	Money: A Suicide Note by Martin Amis
1985	The Handmaid's Tale by Margaret Atwood
1985	White Noise by Don DeLillo
1985	Lake Wobegon Days by Garrison Keillor
1986	It by Stephen King
1986	Wanderlust by Danielle Steele
1987	Patriot Games by Tom Clancy
1987	Beloved by Toni Morrison
1987	The Bonfire of the Vanities by Tom Wolfe
1988	The Cardinal of the Kremlin by Tom Clancy
1988	The Sands of Time by Sidney Sheldon
1989	Clear and Present Danger by Stephen R. Covey
1989	The Pillars of the Earth by Ken Follett

Around the World When You Turned 40

International stories from farflung places—but did they appear on your radar as you clocked up four decades on the planet?

- ✦ Iraq invades Kuwait
- ✦ Yemen becomes one united country
- ✦ Iran hit by 7.4 magnitude earthquake
- ✦ World Wide Web is proposed in Switzerland
- ✦ Lech Walesa becomes president of Poland
- ✦ Burma holds elections but denied by military
- ✦ Ban on trading ivory is proposed
- ✦ Mandela becomes leader of African National Congress
- ✦ Germany reunifies into one country
- ✦ Thatcher resigns as prime minister
- ✦ Stampede at Mecca leaves 1,400 dead
- ✦ Officials close Tower of Pisa to tourists for safety reasons
- ✦ The Philippines is struck by 7.7-magnitude earthquake
- ✦ Gorbachev is awarded Nobel Peace Prize
- ✦ Chunnel workers meet under Channel
- ✦ Namibia gains independence
- ✦ Yeltsin becomes president of Russia
- ✦ West Germany wins World Cup in Italy
- ✦ UK suffers worst heat wave in recorded history
- ✦ Scientists discover new hole in ozone layer
- ✦ UK and Argentina restore diplomatic relations
- ✦ New Zealand navy ends rum ration
- ✦ Imelda Marcos goes on trial
- ✦ Nicaragua elects woman for president
- ✦ Estonia becomes a republic

Across the Nation

Here are the headline stories from across the country in the year you hit 40.

- Panama invaded; Manuel Noriega surrenders to US forces
- McMartin preschool trial ends with all defendants acquitted
- Voyager 1 sends back picture of Earth–"the pale blue dot"
- Upland earthquake hits Los Angeles
- Art theft in Boston results in the largest theft of private property
- Arson at illegal social club kills 87 people
- Hubble Space Telescope launched from Discovery (right)
- Financier Michael Milken pleads guilty
- President Bush and Gorbachev hold summit in Washington
- Lower Ohio Valley tornado outbreak occurs
- President Bush breaks pledge of "No new taxes"
- Americans with Disabilities Act signed
- Ellis Island opens as museum
- Clean Air Act of 1990 passed
- Sue, the most complete skeleton of a T-Rex, is discovered
- Recession strikes US economy
- McDonald's starts cooking fries in vegetable oil
- Microsoft includes Solitaire game to help teach users drag and drop
- Ken Griffey Sr. & Jr. both hit homeruns in the same game
- San Francisco 49ers win Super Bowl
- John Kevorkian assists a woman to commit suicide
- Cal Ripken plays in his 1,308th baseball game
- Comedian Roseanne Barr mangles National Anthem at game
- Operation Desert Shield commences

Born this year:
- Actress Jennifer Lawrence
- Actress Kristen Stewart
- Actress Sarah Hyland

NASA

24 April: space shuttle Discovery lifts off with its precious cargo, the Hubble Space Telescope. This instrument has given scientists a new understanding of the cosmos with its crystal-clear view from an orbit 340 miles above the Earth. The length of a school bus, Hubble is 1,400 kg heavier than it was when it was launched thanks to numerous improvements and enhancements since launch

The Biggest Hits When You Were 40

Big tunes for a big birthday: how many of them enticed your middle-aged party guests onto the dance floor?

Madonna 🎤 Vogue
Garth Brooks 🎤 Friends in Low Places
Alannah Myles 🎤 Black Velvet
Wilson Phillips 🎤 Hold On
Roxette 🎤 It Must Have Been Love
Alabama 🎤 Jukebox in My Mind
Vanilla Ice 🎤 Ice Ice Baby
EMF 🎤 Unbelievable
Bon Jovi 🎤 Blaze of Glory
Patty Loveless 🎤 Chains
Jane's Addiction 🎤 Been Caught Stealing
Sinead O'Connor 🎤 Nothing Compares 2 U
Poison 🎤 Unskinny Bop
Vince Gill 🎤 When I Call Your Name
Bell Biv DeVoe 🎤 Poison
Depeche Mode 🎤 Policy of Truth
Lisa Stansfield 🎤 All Around the World
Kathy Mattea 🎤 Where've You Been
C+C Music Factory 🎤 Gonna Make You Sweat
(Everybody Dance Now)
Billy Idol 🎤 Cradle of Love
MC Hammer 🎤 U Can't Touch This
The B-52s 🎤 Roam
Nelson 🎤 (Can't Live Without Your)
Love and Affection
Technotronic 🎤 Pump Up the Jam

Popular Food in the 1970s

From fads to ads, here's a new collection of dinner party dishes and family favorites. This time it's the seventies that's serving up the delights—and some of us are still enjoying them today!

Watergate Salad
Black Forest cake
Chex Mix
Cheese Tid-Bits
Dolly Madison Koo-koos (cupcakes)

Life Cereal
"I'm not gonna try it. You try it. Let's get Mikey…he hates everything." Three on- and off-screen brothers, one memorable ad that ran for much of the seventies.

The Manwich
"A sandwich is a sandwich, but a manwich is a meal," the ads announced in 1969.

Tomato aspic
Bacardi rum cake
Impossible pies
Zucchini bread
Oscar Mayer bologna
Poke Cake made with Jell-O
Libbyland Dinners

Reggie! Bar
Named after New York Yankees' right fielder Reggie Jackson and launched as a novely, Reggie! Bars were on sale for six years.

Hostess Chocodiles
Polynesian chicken salad
Salmon mousse
Cheese log appetizer
Gray Poupon Dijon Mustard

Tootsie Pop
So how many licks does it take to get to the center of a Tootsie Pop? 364, and that's official: it was tested on a "licking machine."

Cars of the 1970s

A decade of strikes, federal regulations, foreign imports, oil crises, safety and quality concerns: car sales were up overall, but the US industry was under pressure like never before. Iconic new models to debut include the Pontiac Firebird and the outrageous, gold-plated Stutz Blackhawk.

1940	**Chrysler New Yorker**
	When is a New Yorker not a New Yorker? The eighth generation of this upscale car bore little resemblance to the 1940 launch models. Yet in 1970, the New Yorker was barely middle-aged: they lived on until 1997.
1948	Ford F-Series
1959	General Motors Cadillac Coupe de Ville
1959	Chrysler Plymouth Valiant
1960	Chrysler Dodge Dart
1961	**General Motors Oldsmobile Cutlass**
	The Cutlass outsold any other model in US for four consecutive years, notching up nearly 2 million sales.
1962	General Motors Chevrolet Nova
1965	General Motors Chevrolet Caprice
1965	Ford LTD
1967	General Motors Pontiac Firebird
1968	BMW 2002
1970	Chrysler Dodge Challenger
1970	General Motors Chevrolet Monte Carlo
1970	General Motors Chevrolet Vega
1970	American Motors Corporation Hornet
1970	Ford Maverick
1971	Nissan Datsun 240Z
1971	**Stutz Blackhawk**
	These luxury automobiles started at a cool $22,000 ($150,000 today); the first car sold went to Elvis. Among the many other celebrity Blackhawk owners was Dean Martin; one of his three models sported the vanity plate DRUNKY. He crashed it.
1971	Ford Pinto
1973	Honda Civic
1975	Ford Granada
1978	Ford Fiesta

US Banknotes

The cast of US banknotes hasn't changed in your lifetime, giving you plenty of time to get to know them. (Although if you have a lot of pictures of James Madison and Salmon P. Chase around the house, you might want to think about a visit to the bank.)

Fifty cent paper coin (1862-1876) 🖼 Abraham Lincoln
These bills were known as "shinplasters" because the quality of the paper was so poor that they could be used to bandage leg wounds during the Civil War.

One dollar bill (1862-1869) 🖼 Salmon P. Chase
The US Secretary of Treasury during Civil War, Salmon P. Chase is credited with putting the phrase "In God we trust" on US currency beginning in 1864.

One dollar bill (1869-present) 🖼 George Washington
Some bills have a star at the end of the serial number. This means they are replacement bills for those printed with errors.

One silver dollar certificate (1886-96) 🖼 Martha Washington

Two dollar bill (1862-present) 🖼 Thomas Jefferson
Two dollar bills have a reputation of being rare, but there are actually 600 million in circulation in the US.

Five dollar bill (1914-present) 🖼 Abraham Lincoln
Ten dollar bill (1914-1929) 🖼 Andrew Jackson
Ten dollar bill (1929-present) 🖼 Alexander Hamilton
Twenty dollar bill (1865-1869) 🖼 Pocahontas
Twenty dollar bill (1914-1929) 🖼 Grover Cleveland
Twenty dollar bill (1929-present) 🖼 Andrew Jackson
Fifty dollar bill (1914-present) 🖼 Ulysses S. Grant

One hundred dollar bill (1914-1929) 🖼 Benjamin Franklin
The one hundred dollar bill has an expected circulation life of 22.9 years while the one dollar bill has an expected circulation life of just 6.6 years.

Five hundred dollar bill (1918-1928) 🖼 John Marshall
Five hundred dollar bill (1945-1969) 🖼 William McKinley
One thousand dollar bill (1918-1928) 🖼 Alexander Hamilton
One thousand dollar bill (1928-1934) 🖼 Grover Cleveland
Five thousand dollar bill (1918-1934) 🖼 James Madison
Ten thousand dollar bill (1928-1934) 🖼 Salmon P. Chase

Male Olympic Gold Medalists in Your Lifetime

These are the male athletes that have scooped the greatest number of individual and team gold medals at the Summer Olympics in your lifetime.

Michael Phelps (23) 👑 Swimming (right)
Carl Lewis (9) 👑 Athletics
Mark Spitz (9) 👑 Swimming
For 36 years, Spitz's 7-gold-medal haul at the 1972 Munich Olympics was unbeaten; Michael Phelps finally broke the spell with his eighth gold in Beijing.

Matt Biondi (8) 👑 Swimming
Caeleb Dressel (7) 👑 Swimming
Ryan Lochte (6) 👑 Swimming
Don Schollander (5) 👑 Swimming
Gary Hall Jr. (5) 👑 Swimming
Aaron Peirsol (5) 👑 Swimming
Nathan Adrian (5) 👑 Swimming
Tom Jager (5) 👑 Swimming
Al Oerter Jr. (4) 👑 Athletics
Four out of four: Oerter won Olympic gold medals in the discus in every Games from 1956–1968. He fought injuries that required him to wear a neck brace for the 1964 Tokyo Olympics—but he still set an Olympic record.

Greg Louganis (4) 👑 Diving
Jason Lezak (4) 👑 Swimming
John Naber (4) 👑 Swimming
Jon Olsen (4) 👑 Swimming
Lenny Krayzelburg (4) 👑 Swimming
Matt Grevers (4) 👑 Swimming
Michael Johnson (4) 👑 Athletics
Once the fastest man in the world over 200 meters, Johnson took 15 minutes to walk the same distance in 2018 following a mini-stroke—but took it as a sign that he'd make a full recovery.

Between 2000 and 2016, Michael Phelps won 28 Olympic medals, including 23 gold and 16 for individual events. That's 10 more than his nearest competitor, Larisa Latynina, a gymnast of the Soviet Union who took her last gold medal fifty years earlier.

Winter Olympics Venues Since You Were Born

Unless you're an athlete or winter sports fan, the Winter Olympics can slip past almost unnoticed. These are the venues; can you remember the host countries and years?

Lillehammer
Cortina d'Ampezzo
Oslo
Salt Lake City
Sapporo
Albertville
The last Games to be held in the same year as the Summer Olympics, with the next Winter Olympics held two years later.

Turin
Grenoble
Beijing
Sarajevo
Lake Placid
Sochi
Innsbruck (twice)
This usually snowy city experienced its mildest winter in 60 years; the army was called in to transport snow and ice from the mountains. Nevertheless, twelve years later, the Winter Olympics were back.

Squaw Valley
Nagano
Calgary
Vancouver
PyeongChang

Answers: Lillehammer: Norway, 1994; Cortina d'Ampezzo: Italy, 1956; Oslo: Norway, 1952; Salt Lake City: USA, 2002; Sapporo: Japan, 1972; Albertville: France, 1992; Turin: Italy, 2006; Grenoble: France, 1968; Beijing: China, 2022; Sarajevo: Yugoslavia, 1984; Lake Placid: USA, 1980; Sochi: Russia, 2014; Innsbruck: Austria, 1964; Squaw Valley: USA, 1960; Nagano: Japan, 1998; Calgary: Canada, 1988; Innsbruck: Austria, 1976; Vancouver: Canada, 2010; PyeongChang: South Korea, 2018

Fashion in the Eighties

Eighties fashion was many things, but subtle wasn't one of them. Influences were everywhere from aerobics to Wall Street, from pop princesses to preppy polo shirts. The result was chaotic, but fun. How many eighties throwbacks still lurk in your closet?

Stirrup pants
Ralph Lauren
Ruffled shirts
Jean Paul Gaultier
Acid wash jeans
Stone washing had been around a while, but the acid wash trend came about by chance—Rifle jeans of Italy accidentally tumbled jeans, bleach, and pumice stone with a little water. The result? A fashion craze was born.

Camp collar shirt with horizontal stripes
Thierry Mugler
Oversized denim jackets
Scrunchies
"Members Only" jackets
Members Only military-inspired jackets were marketed with the tagline "When you put it on...something happens."

Paper bag waist pants
Pleated stonewash baggy jeans
Cut-off sweatshirts/hoodies
Vivienne Westwood
Azzedine Alaia
Shoulder pads
Dookie chains
Leg warmers
Bally shoes
Jordache jeans
Calvin Klein
Windbreaker jackets
Ray-Ban Wayfarer sunglasses
Popularized by Tom Cruise in the movie Risky Business.

Parachute pants
Jumpsuits

World Buildings

Some of the most striking and significant buildings in the world sprang up when you were between 25 and 50 years old. How many do you know?

1975	First Canadian Place, Toronto
1976	The CN Tower, Toronto
1977	**The Centre Pompidou, Paris**

The Centre Pompidou, known locally as Beaubourg, is considered the "inside-out" landmark—its structure and mechanical services are outside the building.

1978	Sunshine 60, Tokyo
1979	Kuwait Towers, Kuwait City
1980	Hopewell Centre, Hong Kong
1981	Sydney Tower
1982	First Canadian Centre, Calgary
1984	Deutsche Bank Twin Towers, Frankfurt
1985	Exchange Square, Hong Kong
1986	**Baha'i Lotus Temple, New Delhi**

The Lotus Temple is open to all faiths to come worship, but no images, pictures, sermons, or even musical instruments are permitted.

1988	Canterra Tower, Calgary
1989	The Louvre Pyramid, Paris
1990	Bank of China Tower, Hong Kong
1991	One Canada Square, London
1992	Central Plaza, Hong Kong
1994	Shinjuku Park Tower, Tokyo
1995	Republic Plaza, Singapore
1996	**Petronas Twin Towers, Kuala Lampur**

As iconic in Malaysia as the Eiffel Tower is in France. Its skybridge is actually two stories and is the highest of its kind in the world.

1997	Guggenheim Museum Bilbao
1998	City of Arts and Sciences, Valencia
1999	Burj Al Arab, Dubai
2000	Emirates Tower One, Dubai

Kentucky Derby Winners

These are the equine and human heroes from the "most exciting two minutes of sport" during your thirties and forties. Did any of them make you rich?

1980	**Genuine Risk (Jacinto Vasquez)**

Genuine Risk (Jacinto Vasquez)
Genuine Risk became the first female horse to win the Kentucky Derby since 1915.

1981	Pleasant Colony (Jorge Velasquez)
1982	Gato Del Sol (Eddie Delahoussaye)
1983	Sunny's Halo (Eddie Delahoussaye)
1984	Swale (Laffit Pincay Jr.)
1985	Spend A Buck (Angel Cordero Jr.)
1986	**Ferdinand (Bill Shoemaker)**

Ferdinand (Bill Shoemaker)
54-year-old Bill Shoemaker became the oldest jockey to ever win the Kentucky Derby.

1987	Alysheba (Chris McCarron)
1988	Winning Colors (Gary Stevens)
1989	Sunday Silence (Pat Valenzuela)
1990	Unbridled (Craig Perret)
1991	Strike the Gold (Chris Antley)
1992	Lil E. Tee (Pat Day)
1993	Sea Hero (Jerry Bailey)
1994	Go for Gin (Chris McCarron)
1995	Thunder Gulch (Gary Stevens)
1996	Grindstone (Jerry Bailey)
1997	Silver Charm (Gary Stevens)
1998	**Real Quiet (Kent Desormeaux)**

Real Quiet (Kent Desormeaux)
Real Quiet missed out on a Triple Crown by fractions of a second.

| 1999 | Charismatic (Chris Antley) |
| 2000 | Fusaichi Pegasus (Kent Desormeaux) |

World Series Champions Since You Were Born

These are the winners of the Commissioner's Trophy and the number of times they've been victorious in your lifetime.

- ⚾ Detroit Tigers (2)
- ⚾ New York Yankees (14)
- ⚾ Cincinnati Reds (3)
- ⚾ St. Louis Cardinals (5)
- ⚾ New York Giants (1)
- ⚾ Brooklyn Dodgers (1)
- ⚾ Milwaukee Braves (1)
- ⚾ **Los Angeles Dodgers (6)**
  1988: Dodgers' Kirk Gibson, battling injuries, hit a game-winning home run in his only at-bat of the 1988 World Series.
- ⚾ Pittsburgh Pirates (3)
- ⚾ Baltimore Orioles (3)
- ⚾ **New York Mets (2)**
  1969: The Mets had never finished above 9th in their division.
- ⚾ Oakland Athletics (4)
- ⚾ Philadelphia Phillies (2)
- ⚾ Kansas City Royals (2)
- ⚾ **Minnesota Twins (2)**
  1991: Both teams had finished in last place the previous season.
- ⚾ Toronto Blue Jays (2)
- ⚾ Atlanta Braves (2)
- ⚾ Florida Marlins (2)
- ⚾ Arizona Diamondbacks (1)
- ⚾ Anaheim Angels (1)
- ⚾ Boston Red Sox (4)
- ⚾ Chicago White Sox (1)
- ⚾ San Francisco Giants (3)
- ⚾ **Chicago Cubs (1)**
  2016: The Cubs' first World Series win since 1908.
- ⚾ Houston Astros (1)
- ⚾ Washington Nationals (1)

Books of the Decade

By our forties, most of us have decided what we like to read. But occasionally a book can break the spell, revealing the delights of other genres. Did any of these newly published books do that for you?

1990	The Plains of Passage by Jean M. Auel
1990	Possession by A.S. Byatt
1990	Four Past Midnight by Stephen King
1991	The Firm by John Grisham
1991	The Kitchen God's Wife by Amy Tan
1991	Scarlett by Alexandra Ripley
1992	The Bridges of Madison County by Robert James Waller
1992	The Secret History by Donna Tartt
1993	The Celestine Prophecy by James Redfield
1993	Like Water for Chocolate by Laura Esquivel
1994	The Chamber by John Grisham
1994	Disclosure by Michael Crichton
1995	The Horse Whisperer by Nicholas Evans
1995	The Lost World by Michael Crichton
1995	The Rainmaker by John Grisham
1996	Angela's Ashes by Frank McCourt
1996	Bridget Jones's Diary by Helen Fielding
1996	Infinite Jest by David Foster Wallace
1997	American Pastoral by Philip Roth
1997	Tuesdays with Morrie by Mitch Albom
1998	The Poisonwood Bible by Barbara Kingsolver
1998	A Man in Full by Tom Wolfe
1999	The Testament by John Grisham
1999	Hannibal by Thomas Harris
1999	Girl with a Pearl Earring by Tracy Chevalier

Vice Presidents in Your Lifetime

The linchpin of a successful presidency, the best springboard to become POTUS, or both? Here are the men—and woman—who have shadowed the most powerful person in the world in your lifetime.

1949-53	**Alben W. Barkley** Barkley died of a heart attack during a convention speech three years after the end of his term.
1953-61	Richard Nixon
1961-63	Lyndon B. Johnson
1965-69	**Hubert Humphrey** Christmas 1977: with just weeks to live, the former VP to President Johnson made goodbye calls. One was to Richard Nixon, the man who had beaten Humphrey to become president in 1968. Sensing Nixon's unhappiness at his status as Washington outcast, Humphrey invited him to take a place of honor at a funeral he knew was fast approaching.
1969-73	**Spiro Agnew (right)**
1973-74	Gerald Ford
1974-77	Nelson Rockefeller
1977-81	Walter Mondale
1981-89	**George H. W. Bush** He is only the second vice president to win the presidency while holding the office of vice president.
1989-93	**Dan Quayle** Quayle famously misspelled potato ("potatoe")
1993-2001	**Al Gore** This VP won the Nobel Peace Prize in 2007, following in the footsteps of two other former vice presidents.
2001-09	Dick Cheney
2009-17	Joe Biden
2017-20	**Mike Pence** In the 90s, Pence took a break from politics to become a conservative radio talk show and television host.
2020-	Kamala Harris

Mary Evans / Everett Collection

Spiro Agnew resigned in 1973, the second VP to quit in America's history (the first was John Calhoun in 1932). He stepped down after being charged with tax evasion and taking bribes. He covered his legal debts with a loan from friend Frank Sinatra. In 1983 he was compelled to repay $268,000: the money he had taken in bribes, plus interest.

British Prime Ministers in Your Lifetime

These are the occupants of 10 Downing Street, London, during your lifetime (not including Larry the resident cat). Don't be deceived by that unassuming black (blast-proof) door: Number 10 features a warren of more than 100 rooms.

1945-51	Clement Attlee
1951-55	**Sir Winston Churchill** Churchill was made an honorary citizen of the United States in 1963, one of only eight to receive this honor.
1955-57	Sir Anthony Eden
1957-63	**Harold Macmillan** Macmillan was the scion of a wealthy publishing family. He resigned following a scandal in which a minister was found to have lied about his relationship with a 19-year-old model. Macmillan died aged 92; his last words were, "I think I will go to sleep now."
1963-64	Sir Alec Douglas-Home
1964-70	Harold Wilson
1970-74	Edward Heath
1974-76	Harold Wilson
1976-79	James Callaghan
1979-90	**Margaret Thatcher** In 1994, Thatcher was working late in a Brighton hotel, preparing a conference speech. A bomb—planted weeks earlier by the IRA five stories above—detonated, devastating the hotel. Five were killed; Thatcher was unscathed. The conference went ahead.
1990-97	John Major
1997-2007	Tony Blair
2007-10	**Gordon Brown** Brown has no sight in his left eye after being kicked in a school rugby game; in 2009, while Prime Minister, rips in the right retina were also diagnosed.
2010-16	David Cameron
2016-19	Theresa May
2019-	Boris Johnson

Things People Do Now (Part 2)

Imagine your ten-year-old self being given this list of today's mundane tasks and habits—and the puzzled look on your face!

+ Listen to a podcast
+ Go "viral" or become social media famous
+ Watch YouTube
+ Track the exact location of family members via your smartphone
+ Watch college football playoffs
+ Have drive-thru fast food delivered to your door
+ Check reviews before trying a new restaurant or product
+ Use LED light bulbs to save on your electric bill
+ Wear leggings as pants for any occasion
+ Use hashtags (#) to express an idea or show support
+ Join a CrossFit gym
+ Use a Forever stamp to send a letter
+ Carry a reusable water bottle
+ Work for a company with an "unlimited" paid time off policy
+ "Binge" a TV show
+ Marry a person of the same sex
+ Take your shoes off when going through airport security
+ Take a selfie
+ Use tooth-whitening strips
+ Feed babies and kids from food pouches
+ Buy recreational marijuana from a dispensary (in some states)
+ Store documents "in the cloud" and work on them from any device
+ Clean up after your pets using compostable waste bags
+ Buy free-range eggs and meat at the grocery store

A Lifetime of Technology

It's easy to lose sight of the breadth and volume of life-enhancing technology that became commonplace during the 20th Century. Here are some of the most notable advances to be made in the years you've been an adult.

1971	Email
1972	Video games console (Magnavox Odyssey)
1973	Mobile phone
1974	Universal Product Code
1976	Apple Computer
1979	Compact disc
1981	Graphic User Interface (GUI)
1982	**Emoticons** The inventor of the smiley emoticon hands out "Smiley" cookies every September 19th—the anniversary of the first time it was used.
1983	Internet
1983	Microsoft Word
1984	LCD projector
1988	**Internet virus** The first Internet worm was specifically designed to crack passwords. Its inventor was the son of the man who invented computer passwords.
1989	World Wide Web
1992	Digital hand-sized mobile phone
1994	Bluetooth
1995	**Mouse with scroll wheel** Mouse scroll wheels were developed primarily as a zoom function for large Excel sheets, but became more useable as a means of scrolling.
1998	Google
1999	Wi-Fi
2000	Camera phone
2001	Wikipedia
2004	Facebook
2007	Apple iPhone
2009	Bitcoin
2014	Amazon Alexa

The Biggest Hits When You Were 50

Fifty: an age when your musical taste is largely settled and modern music can lose its appeal…but how many do you know and how many do you like?

Madonna 🎵 Music
Santana featuring
The Product G&B 🎵 Maria Maria
Macy Gray 🎵 I Try
The Dixie Chicks 🎵 Cowboy Take Me Away
Bon Jovi 🎵 It's My Life
Creed 🎵 Higher
Lee Ann Womack 🎵 I Hope You Dance
Blink-182 🎵 All the Small Things
Destiny's Child 🎵 Say My Name
3 Doors Down 🎵 Kryptonite
Metallica 🎵 No Leaf Clover
Faith Hill 🎵 The Way You Love Me
Pink 🎵 There You Go
Red Hot Chili Peppers 🎵 Otherside
LeAnn Rimes 🎵 I Need You
Keith Urban 🎵 Your Everything
Everclear 🎵 Wonderful
Eiffel 65 🎵 Blue (Da Ba Dee)
Keith Urban 🎵 Your Everything
Britney Spears 🎵 Oops!... I Did It Again
Rascal Flatts 🎵 Prayin' for Daylight
Kid Rock 🎵 Only God Knows Why
Third Eye Blind 🎵 Never Let You Go
Eminem 🎵 The Real Slim Shady

Grand Constructions

Governments around the world spent much of the 20th century nation building (and rebuilding), with huge civil engineering projects employing new construction techniques. Here are some of the biggest built between the ages of 25 and 50.

1975	Orange-Fish River Tunnel, South Africa
1976	**Sonnenberg Tunnel, Switzerland** A 5,000-ft road tunnel built to double up as a 20,000-capacity nuclear shelter. Blast doors weigh 350 tons... but take 24 hours to close.
1977	Guoliang Tunnel, China
1978	West Gate Bridge, Australia
1980	Reichsbrücke, Austria
1981	Tjörn Bridge, Scandanavia
1982	Abu Dhabi International Airport, Abu Dhabi
1983	Queen Alia International Airport, Jordan
1984	Tennessee-Tombigbee Waterway, US
1986	National Waterway 1, India
1987	Pikeville Cut-Through, US
1988	Great Seto Bridge, Japan
1989	Skybridge (TransLink), Canada
1990	Ningbo Lishe International Airport, China
1991	Fannefjord Tunnel, Norway
1992	Vidyasagar Setu Bridge, India
1993	Rainbow Bridge, Japan
1994	**English Channel tunnel, UK & France** Even at its predicted cost of $7 billion, the longest underwater tunnel in the world was already the most expensive project ever. By the time it opened, the bill was more than $13 billion.
1995	Denver International Airport, US
1997	British Library, UK
1998	SuperTerminal 1, Hong Kong
1999	**Northstar Island, US** Northstar is a five-acre artificial island created off Prudhoe Bay, Alaska. Pack ice means a conventional floating platform can't be used; during construction, an ice road brought in supplies.

Popular Food in the 1980s

The showy eighties brought us food to dazzle and delight. Food to make us feel good, food to share and food to go. Some innovations fell by the wayside, but many more can still be found in our baskets forty years later.

Hot Pockets
Hot Pockets were the brainchild of two brothers, originally from Iran. Their invention was launched as the Tastywich before being tweaked to become the Hot Pockets enjoyed by millions.

Bagel Bites
Crystal Light
Steak-Umms
Sizzlean Bacon
Potato skins appetizers
Tofutti ice cream

Hi-C Ecto Cooler
Hi-C has been around for a very long time, but the Ecto Cooler dates back to the Ghostbusters movie hype of the 1980s.

Hot buttered O's
Knorr Spinach Dip
Original New York Seltzer
Blondies

Blackened Redfish
The trend for blackening redfish prompted fish stocks to drop so low that commercial fishing for the species was banned in Louisiana.

Bartles & Jaymes Wine Coolers
Fruit Wrinkles
Stuffed mushrooms appetizers

TCBY Frozen Yogurt
TCBY originally stood for "This Can't Be Yogurt."

Sushi
Fajitas
Capri Sun
Jell-O Pudding Pops

Lean Cuisine frozen meals
Lean Cuisine is an FDA-regulated term, so all Lean Cuisine frozen meals need to be within the limit for saturated fat and cholesterol.

Eighties Symbols of Success

In the flamboyant era of Dallas and Dynasty there were many ways to show that you, too, had really made it. Forty years on, it's fascinating to see how some of these throwbacks are outdated or available to nearly everyone, while others are still reserved for today's wealthy peacocks.

BMW car
Cellular car phone
Rolex watch
Cosmetic surgery
In 1981 there were 1,000 liposuction procedures performed. That number increased to 250,000 by 1989.

VCR
"Home theater" projection TV
In-ground pool
AKC-registered dog
McMansion
Pagers/"beeper"
Aprica stroller
Home intercom system
Heart-shaped Jacuzzi tub
NordicTrack
This machine was originally called the Nordic Jock but was renamed due to compaints from women's rights groups.

Cruise vacation
Restaurant-standard kitchen appliances
A popular commercial stove produced enough heat to warm an average three-bedroom home. It was the energy equivalent of six residential stoves.

Ronald Reagan-style crystal jelly bean jar on your desk
Apple or Commodore 64 home computer
Volvo Station Wagon
Gordon Gekko-style "power suit"
Owning a horse or riding lessons for your children
Private jet
Tennis bracelet
Monogrammed clothes and accessories

Launched in 1980, the Apple III personal computer seen here went on sale for a hefty $4,000 and up, the equivalent of over $13,000 today. It didn't sell well and was soon withdrawn (unlike the Apple II, which went on to sell more than 5 million units).

The Transportation Coils

This novel issue of more than 50 definitive stamps first appeared on post in the early eighties, and became a favorite of collectors for its mono color engraved images of transportation methods past and present. Stamps carrying the printing plate number are particularly treasured. Here's a selection you may remember.

1 c 🔲 Omnibus
2 c 🔲 Locomotive
3 c 🔲 Handcar
4 c 🔲 **Stagecoach**

Coaches have been ferrying people and mail between US towns and cities since the late 18th century.

5 c 🔲 Motorcycle
5.5c 🔲 **Star Route Truck**

Star routes were 19th century mail routes on which carriers bid to make deliveries.

6 c 🔲 Tricycle
7.4 c 🔲 Baby Buggy
10 c 🔲 Canal Boat
11 c 🔲 Caboose
12.5 c 🔲 Pushcart
13 c 🔲 Patrol Wagon
15 c 🔲 Tugboat
17 c 🔲 Electric Auto
17 c 🔲 Dog Sled
17.5 c 🔲 Racing car
18 c 🔲 Surrey
20 c 🔲 Cog Railway
21 c 🔲 Railway Mail Car
23 c 🔲 Lunch Wagon
24.1 c 🔲 Tandem Bike
25 c 🔲 Bread Wagon
32 c 🔲 Ferry Boat
$1 🔲 **Sea Plane**

The US Navy bought its first sea plane in 1911: a Curtiss Model E, with a range of 150 miles.

Eighties Game Shows

By the eighties, game shows had their work cut out to compete against the popularity of new drama and talk shows. Still, an injection of celebrity glamour and dollar bills—alongside hours to be filled on new cable TV channels—ensured their survival. Here are the biggies.

Double Dare 🏆 (1986-2019)
Remote Control 🏆 (1987-90)
Scrabble 🏆 (1984-93)
The Price Is Right 🏆 (1972-present)
"Come on down!"—perhaps the best-known game show catchphrase of all time. One 2008 contestant was even happier than usual to do just that after 3 chips dropped into the Plinko all hit the $10,000 jackpot. Fluke? No, wires used to rig the result when filming ads hadn't been removed. She was allowed to keep the $30,000.

Family Feud 🏆 (1976-present)
Press Your Luck 🏆 (1983-86)
A show perhaps best remembered for the contestant Michael Larson, who memorized the game board and engineered a winning streak worth over $110,000. It wasn't cheating—Larson kept the winnings—but the game was swiftly reformulated.

Chain Reaction 🏆 1980-present)
Blockbusters 🏆 (1980-87)
Win, Lose, or Draw 🏆 (1987-90)
On The Spot 🏆 (1984-88)
Jeopardy! 🏆 (1964-present)
Card Sharks 🏆 (1978-present)
Wheel of Fortune 🏆 (1975-present)
Hostess Vanna White is estimated to clap 600 times a show; that's around 4,000,000 times since she began in 1982.

Fandango 🏆 (1983-88)
Body Language 🏆 (1984-86)
Jackpot! 🏆 (1974-90)

Popular Boys' Names

Not many of these boys' names were popular when you were born. But how many more of them are now in your twenty-first century family?

Jacob
Ethan
Michael
Jayden
This is Jayden's highest ever ranking which he'll keep for one more year, before sliding out of favor.

William
Alexander
Noah
Daniel
Aiden
Anthony
Joshua
Mason
Christopher
Andrew
David
Matthew
Logan
Elijah
James
Joseph
Gabriel
Benjamin
Ryan
Samuel
Jackson
John

Rising and falling stars:
Jaxon and Bentley are in; Aidan, Eric and Bryan are out.

Popular Girls' Names

It's a similar story for girls' names: only Elizabeth featured in the 30 most popular names for your year of birth. How long will it be before we turn full circle and Shirley, Patricia and Barbara make a comeback?

Isabella
Isabella's two years in pole position didn't come close to Mary's time at the top in the years since 1900 (54 years). Others: Linda (6), Lisa (8), Jennifer (15), Jessica (9), Ashley (2), Emma (6), Emily (12), Sophia (3) and Olivia (since 2019).

Sophia
Emma
Olivia
Ava
Emily
Abigail
Madison
Chloe
Mia
Addison
Elizabeth
Ella
Natalie
Samantha
Alexis
Lily
Grace
Hailey
Hannah
Alyssa
Lillian
Avery
Leah

Rising and falling stars:
Say hello to Naomi; wave goodbye to Jessica, Angelina, Gabrielle, Valeria, Rachel and Paige.

Game Show Hosts of the Seventies and Eighties

Here is the new generation of hosts: bow-tied, wide-smiled men to steer family favorites through tumultuous times. Astonishingly, one or two are still holding the cards.

John Charles Daly ➤◆ What's My Line (1950–1967)
Garry Moore ➤◆ To Tell The Truth (1969–1976)
Chuck Woolery ➤◆ Love Connection (1983–1994)
Bob Barker ➤◆ The Price Is Right (1972–2007)
Pat Sajak ➤◆ Wheel of Fortune (1981–)
Sajak took the crown for the longest-reigning game-show host of all time in 1983, when his 35-year reign surpassed that of Bob Barker as host of The Price is Right.

Peter Tomarken ➤◆ Press Your Luck (1983–86)
Gene Rayburn ➤◆ The Match Game (1962–1981)
Alex Trebek ➤◆ Jeopardy! (1984–2020)
At the time of his death in 2020, Trebek had hosted more than 8,200 episodes of the show.

Dick Clark ➤◆ Pyramid (1973–1988)
Richard Dawson ➤◆ Family Feud (1976–1995)
Peter Marshall ➤◆ Hollywood Squares (1966–1981)
Howard Cosell ➤◆ Battle of the Network Stars (1976–1988)
Marc Summers ➤◆ Double Dare (1986–1993)
Tom Kennedy ➤◆ Name That Tune (1974–1981)
Bert Convy ➤◆ Tattletales (1974–78; 1982–84)
Ken Ober ➤◆ Remote Control (1987–1990)
Jim Lange ➤◆ The Dating Game (1965–1980)
Wink Martindale ➤◆ Tic-Tac-Dough (1978–1985)
Art Fleming ➤◆ Jeopardy! (1964–1975; 1978–79)
Host for the original version, Fleming declined to host the comeback in 1983. His friend Pat Sajak took the job.

Jack Narz ➤◆ Concentration (1973–78)
Dennis James ➤◆ The Price Is Right (1972–77)
Jim Perry ➤◆ $ale of the Century (1983–89)
John Davidson ➤◆ Hollywood Squares (1986–89)
Ray Combs ➤◆ Family Feud (1988–1994)
Mike Adamle ➤◆ American Gladiators (1989–1996)

TV News Anchors of the Seventies and Eighties

The explosion in cable channels that began with CNN in 1980 brought a host of fresh presenters to join the ranks of trusted personalities that bring us the news. How many of them do you remember?

Dan Rather ♟ (CBS)
"Kenneth, what's the frequency?" Those were the words of the man who attacked Rather in 1986. It took a decade before the message was decoded; his assailant wanted to block the beams he believed TV networks were using to target him.

Peter Jennings ♟ (ABC)
Tom Brokaw ♟ (NBC)
Ted Koppel ♟ (ABC)
Bill Beutel ♟ (ABC)
Jessica Savitch ♟ (NBC)
Connie Chung ♟ (NBC)
Diane Sawyer ♟ (CBS/ABC)
Sam Donaldson ♟ (ABC)
Barbara Walters ♟ (ABC)
Walters was a popular pioneer; the first woman to co-host and anchor news programs, reaching 74 million viewers with her interview of Monica Lewinsky.

Frank Reynolds ♟ (ABC)
Jane Pauley ♟ (NBC)
Roger Grimsby ♟ (ABC)
Roger Mudd ♟ (CBS/NBC)
Garrick Utley ♟ (NBC)
Bernard Shaw ♟ (CNN)
Frank McGee ♟ (NBC)
Ed Bradley ♟ (CBS)
Larry King ♟ (CNN)
Kathleen Sullivan ♟ (ABC/CBS/NBC)
Jim Lehrer ♟ (PBS)
Robert MacNeil ♟ (PBS)
In 1963, MacNeil had a brief exchange of words with a man leaving the Texas School Book Depository; to this day, it is uncertain whether this was Lee Harvey Oswald.

FIFA World Cup: Down to the Last Four in Your Life

Here are the teams that have made the last four of the world's most watched sporting event in your lifetime (last year in brackets). The US men's team has reached the semifinals once, back in 1930.

France ⚽ (2018, winner)
Croatia ⚽ (2018, runner-up)
During a 2006 match against Australia, Croatian player Josip Šimunić was booked three times due to a referee blunder.

Belgium ⚽ (2018, 3rd)
England ⚽ (2018, 4th)
In the run-up to the 1966 World Cup, hosted and won by England, the trophy was held to ransom. An undercover detective with fake banknotes arrested the crook; a dog named Pickles found the trophy under a bush.

Brazil ⚽ (2014, 4th)
Germany ⚽ (2014, winner)
Argentina ⚽ (2014, runner-up)
Netherlands ⚽ (2014, 3rd)
Spain ⚽ (2010, winner)
Uruguay ⚽ (2010, 4th)
Italy ⚽ (2006, winner)
Portugal ⚽ (2006, 4th)
Turkey ⚽ (2002, 3rd)
Korean Republic ⚽ (2002, 4th)
Sweden ⚽ (1994, 3rd)
Bulgaria ⚽ (1994, 4th)
Poland ⚽ (1982, 3rd)
Russia ⚽ (1966, 4th)
Czech Republic (as Czechoslovakia) ⚽ (1962, runner-up)
Chile ⚽ (1962, 3rd)
The 1962 World Cup saw the 'Battle of Santiago' between Chile and Italy. The first foul occurred 12 seconds into the game, a player was punched in the nose, and police intervened several times.

Serbia (as Yugoslavia) ⚽ (1962, 4th)
Hungary ⚽ (1954, runner-up)
Austria ⚽ (1954, third)

Books of the Decade

Our final decade of books are the bookstore favorites from your fifties. How many did you read…and can you remember the plot, or the cover?

2000	Angels & Demons by Dan Brown
2000	Interpreter of Maladies by Jhumpa Lahiri
2000	White Teeth by Zadie Smith
2001	Life of Pi by Yann Martel
2001	The Corrections by Jonathan Franzen
2002	Everything is Illuminated by Jonathan Safran Foer
2002	The Lovely Bones by Alice Sebold
2003	The Da Vinci Code by Dan Brown
2003	The Kite Runner by Khaled Hosseini
2004	The Five People You Meet in Heaven by Mitch Albom
2004	Cloud Atlas by David Mitchell
2005	Never Let Me Go by Kazuo Ishiguro
2005	The Book Thief by Markus Zusak
2005	Twilight by Stephanie Meyer
2006	The Secret by Rhonda Byrne
2006	Eat, Pray, Love by Elizabeth Gilbert
2006	The Road by Cormac McCarthy
2007	A Thousand Splendid Suns by Khaled Hosseini
2007	City of Bones by Cassandra Clare
2008	The Hunger Games by Suzanne Collins
2008	The Girl with the Dragon Tattoo by Stieg Larsson
2009	Catching Fire by Suzanne Collins
2009	The Lost Symbol by Dan Brown
2009	The Help by Kathryn Stockett

April 17, 1970: Jim Lovell is brought aboard a helicopter—the last of the three astronauts from the Apollo 13 mission to be lifted from the floating

Apollo Astronauts

Whatever your personal memories of the events, the moon landings are now woven into our national story—but not all of the Apollo astronauts who made the journey are equally well known. Twelve landed; twelve remained in lunar orbit. Gus Grissom, Ed White, and Roger B Chaffee died in training.

Landed on the moon:
Alan Bean
Alan Shepard
Shepard was the oldest person to walk on the moon at age 47.

Buzz Aldrin
Charles Duke
David Scott
Edgar Mitchell
Eugene Cernan
Harrison Schmitt
James Irwin
John Young
Neil Armstrong
Pete Conrad
Remained in low orbit:
Al Worden
Bill Anders
Anders took the iconic "Earthrise" photo.

Dick Gordon
Frank Borman
Fred Haise
Jack Swigert
Jim Lovell
Ken Mattingly
Michael Collins
Ron Evans
Made the final spacewalk of the program to retrieve film cassettes.

Stuart Roosa
On the Apollo 14 mission he carried seeds from 5 species of trees. They were planted across the US and are known as "Moon Trees."

Tom Stafford

US Open Tennis

And now it's the women's turn. Here are the tournament's victors when you were between the ages of the current "winning window": 16 years (Tracy Austin in 1979), and a venerable 42 years (Molla Mallory in 1926: she won eight times).

1966	Maria Bueno
1967	Billie Jean King
1968	Virginia Wade
1969-70	**Margaret Court** Court won both the amateur and open championships in 1969.
1971-72	Billie Jean King
1973	**Margaret Court** In 1973, the US Open became the first Grand Slam tournament to offer equal prize money to male and female winners.
1974	Billie Jean King
1975-78	**Chris Evert** During the 1975 US Open, Evert beat her long-time rival Martina Navratilova in the semi-final. That evening, Navratilova defected to the United States.
1979	**Tracy Austin** 16-year-old Tracy Austin is the youngest US Open champion ever.
1980	Chris Evert
1981	Tracy Austin
1982	Chris Evert
1983-84	Martina Navratilova
1985	Hana Mandikova
1986-87	**Martina Navratilova** The four US Open finalists in 1986 (male and female) were all born in Czechoslovakia.
1988-89	Steffi Graf
1990	Gabriela Sabatini
1991-92	Monica Seles

Things People Did When You Were Growing Up (Part 2)

Finally, here are more of the things we did and errands we ran as kids that nobody needs, wants, or even understands how to do in the modern age!

- ✦ Buy cigarettes for your parents at the corner store as a child
- ✦ Use a pay phone (there was one on almost every corner)
- ✦ Join a bowling league
- ✦ Collect cigarette or baseball trading cards
- ✦ Get frozen meals delivered to your door by the iconic refrigerated yellow Schwan's truck
- ✦ Attend "Lawn Faiths"/ ice cream socials
- ✦ Chat with strangers over CB radio
- ✦ Look up a phone number in the Yellow or White Pages
- ✦ Visit the Bookmobile for new library books
- ✦ Have a radio repaired at an appliance/electronics shop
- ✦ Ride your bike without a helmet
- ✦ Go to American Bandstand parties
- ✦ Take part in a panty raid prank
- ✦ Attend a sock hop
- ✦ Get milk delivered to your door
- ✦ Hang out with friends at a pizzeria
- ✦ Use a rotary phone at home
- ✦ Use a typewriter
- ✦ Save your term paper on a floppy disc
- ✦ Listen to LPs and the newest 45s
- ✦ Care for a pet rock
- ✦ Use a card catalogue to find books at the library
- ✦ Attend a Sadie Hawkins Dance where girls invited the boys
- ✦ Go disco roller skating

Made in the USA
Monee, IL
22 December 2022

23233986R00065